THE LORE OF THE CORPS

Quotations By, For & About Marines

Compiled by MSgt A. A. Bufalo USMC (Ret)

Copyright © 2006 by S&B Publishing

ISBN 978-0-9745793-6-8

First Printing – June 2006
Printed in the United States of America

www.AllAmericanBooks.com

The Lore of the Corps

BOOKS BY ANDY BUFALO

SWIFT, SILENT & SURROUNDED
Sea Stories and Politically Incorrect Common Sense

THE OLDER WE GET, THE BETTER WE WERE
MORE Sea Stories and Politically Incorrect Common Sense
Book II

NOT AS LEAN, NOT AS MEAN, STILL A MARINE!
However, Neither is Marine Corps Policy
Even MORE Sea Stories and Politically Incorrect Common Sense
Book III

EVERY DAY IS A HOLIDAY
Every Meal is a Feast
Yet Another Book of Sea Stories and Politically Incorrect Common Sense
Book IV

THE ONLY EASY DAY WAS YESTERDAY
Fighting the War on Terrorism

HARD CORPS
The Legends of the Marine Corps

AMBASSADORS IN BLUE
In Every Clime and Place
Marine Security Guards Protecting Our Embassies Around the World

SALTY LANGUAGE
An Unabridged Dictionary of Marine Corps Slang, Terms & Jargon

The Lore of the Corps

"Take courage then, seize the fortune that awaits you, repair to the Marine Rendezvous where, in a flowing bowl of punch, and three times three, you shall drink." - *From a Revolutionary War era recruiting poster*

The Lore of the Corps

PREFACE

This compilation of quotes was designed to put all the accolades, wit, wisdom and remarks pertinent to the Marine Corps and the practice of leadership into one volume. Many of them will be familiar, and many will be read for the first time – but they will all stimulate, fascinate and motivate!

In order to get the most out of this book I recommend readers do more than simply "skim" through the entries. Read each one carefully, think it over, and take the time to "digest" what it is telling you. You may be surprised by what you take away from the exercise. I know I was.

Lore was divided into several sections in order to make it easier to locate a particular quote, and you will find some of them listed in multiple sections of the book. This "cross-referencing" was done intentionally in order to further simplify the process of locating a favorite entry. There are also a number of "Non-Marine" quotes included for their value as leadership tools – and since the hallmark of the Corps is great leadership, we have sort of "adopted" them.

I hope you enjoy reading and sharing this book of wit and wisdom as much as I enjoyed compiling it.

Semper Fi,
The Top

The Lore of the Corps

TABLE OF CONTENTS

The Lore of the Corps

QUOTES ABOUT MARINES & THE MARINE CORPS

The Lore of the Corps

"There are only two types of people who understand Marines – the Marines themselves, and the enemy. Everyone else has a second hand opinion." - *General William Thornson, U.S. Army*

"Will Rogers once said the art of diplomacy was saying 'nice doggy' until you could find a rock. Well, the USMC is a nice big rock." - *Earl & Norma Goudie*

"Marine Corps spirit and purpose define American resolve and intent." – *Carrol Childers, a civilian employee at Quantico's Amphibious Warfare School*

"It's great to be here with the greatest of the great, and the strongest of the strong... I only play an action hero, but you people are the *true* action heroes." – *Governor Arnold Schwarzenegger, at a Marine Corps Birthday Ball in Tokyo*

"If forty-five years of a full life never presented a prouder moment than watching your son confidently march across the parade deck on graduation day at Parris Island or San Diego... then you are definitely the very proud parent of a U. S. Marine." – *'Marine Mom' Kolette Abell*

"The story of the self-sacrifice of Major Ortiz and his Marines has become a brilliant legend in that section of France where acts of bravery were considered commonplace." – *Part of Navy Cross citation for Major Pierre J. Ortiz, USMC*

"(They) ran curiously to type, with drilled shoulders and a bone-deep sunburn, and a tolerant scorn of nearly everything on earth. Their speech was flavored with Navy words, and words culled from all the folk who live on the seas and ports where our warships go... They were the Leathernecks, the Old Timers: collected from ship's guards and shore stations all over the earth to form the 4th Brigade of Marines, the two rifle regiments, detached from the Navy by order of the President for service with the American Expeditionary Forces. They were the old breed of American regular, regarding their service at home and at war as an occupation; and they transmitted their temper and character and view-point to the high-hearted volunteer mass which filled the ranks of the Marine Brigade." - *Captain John W. Thompson Jr., describing the men of the 4th Marine Brigade as they prepared for action at Belleau Wood in June of 1918*

"Do Korea's politicians and people know that the Marines who are conducting dangerous combat operations every day in Iraq belong to the *same* Marine division which saved Korea fifty years ago?" - *Lee Sang-don*

"All (Marines) speak the language of the rifle and bayonet, of muddy boots and long, hot marches. It's never 'us and them,' only 'us.' That is the secret of the Corps." - *Colonel Daniel F. Bolger, U.S. Army*

"There is no better group of fighting men anywhere in the world than in the Marine Corps." - *Senator Irving M. Ives*

"The Corps, which has never lost sight that its primary mission is to fight, remains superbly trained and disciplined - true to its time-honored slogan, 'We don't promise you a rose garden.'" - *Colonel David Hackworth, U.S. Army (Ret)*

"Marines walk up and down concrete steps that are literally stenciled with words to live by: 'honor, commitment, duty, fidelity, courage, respect.' They talk about these words, and try to live up to them." - *Kathryn Roth-Douquet*

"They are America's Warriors, and they are ready. These are United States Marines, and they are dangerous. They are poised, if and when the order comes, to wreak havoc on the enemies of their country." – *Phil McCombs, Washington Post, September 13, 2001*

"During the Korean War, Chinese military propagandists told their troops that in order to join the U. S. Marine Corps you had to bring your Mother's head to the recruiter in order to demonstrate your desire to join!"

"Do not attack the 1st Marine Division. They fight like devils. Strike the American Army." - *Chinese Army directive during the Korean War*

"Some people spend an entire lifetime wondering if they made a difference in the world. But, the Marines don't have that problem." - *President Ronald Reagan, 1985*

"The quicker we clean up this damn mess, the quicker we can take a little jaunt against the purple pissing Japs and clean out their nest too, before the Marines get all the damn credit." - *General George S. Patton, close to the end of the war in Europe*

"The Marine pilots were superb. They would fly down a gun barrel." - *LtCmdr Edgar Hoaglund U.S. Navy, Philippines 1945*

"Marines know how to use their bayonets. Army bayonets may as well be paper-weights." - *From a article in the Navy Times; November 1994*

"Marines I see as two breeds, Rottweilers or Dobermans, because Marines come in two varieties, big and mean, or skinny and mean. They're aggressive on the attack, and tenacious on defense. They've got really short hair, and they always go for the throat." - *Rear Admiral "Jay" R. Stark, U.S. Navy; 10 November 1995*

"Lying offshore, ready to act, the presence of ships and Marines sometimes means much more than just having air power or ship's fire, when it comes to deterring a crisis. And the ships and Marines may not have to do anything but lie offshore. It is hard to lie offshore with a C-141 or C-130 full of airborne troops." - *General Colin Powell, U. S. Army, Chairman of the Joint Chiefs of Staff*

"Marines divide the world into two classes: Marines, and those who aren't good enough to be Marines." - *David B. Wood*

"The United States Marine Corps, with its fiercely proud tradition of excellence in combat, its hallowed rituals, and its unbending code of honor, is part of the fabric of American Myth." - *Thomas E. Ricks from "Making the Corps"*

"The Marines I have seen around the world have the cleanest bodies, the filthiest minds, the highest morale, and the lowest morals of any group of animals I have ever seen. Thank God for the United States Marine Corps!" - *First Lady Eleanor Roosevelt, 1945 (Her own son James was a Marine officer)*

"The eyes of the nation and the eyes of the entire world, the eyes of history itself, are on that brave little band of defenders who hold the pass at Khe Sahn." - *President Lyndon Johnson*

"I have just returned from visiting the Marines at the front, and there is not a finer fighting organization in the world! - *General of the Army Douglas MacArthur; Korea, 1950*

"You cannot exaggerate about the Marines. They are convinced to the point of arrogance, that they are the most ferocious fighters on earth - and the amusing thing about it is that they are." - *Father Kevin Keaney, 1st Marine Division Chaplain, Korean War*

"The Marines have landed, and the situation is well in hand." - *Richard Harding Davis*

"Once again I feel the end is near - at least for me... I wonder if I ever had what it takes to be a Marine, and conclude that I never did, and I don't now."- *Newsweek correspondent Arnaud de Borchgrave in Vietnam, October 10, 1966*

"Marines are about the most peculiar breed of human beings I have ever witnessed. They treat their service as if it were some kind of cult, plastering their emblem on almost everything they own, making themselves up to look like insane fanatics with haircuts to ungentlemanly lengths, worshipping their Commandant almost as if he were a god, and making weird animal noises like a band of savages. They'll fight like rabid dogs at the drop of a hat just for the sake of a little action, and are the cockiest sons of bitches I have ever known. Most have the foulest mouths and drink well beyond man's normal limits, but their high spirits and sense of brotherhood set them apart and, generally speaking, the United States Marines I've come in contact with are the most professional soldiers and the finest men I have ever had the pleasure to meet." - *An Anonymous Canadian Citizen*

"I can never again see a United States Marine without experiencing a feeling of reverence." - *General Johnson, U.S. Army*

"The deadliest weapon in the world is a Marine and his rifle." - *General John "Blackjack" Pershing, U.S. Army*

"The safest place in Korea was right behind a platoon of Marines. Lord, how they could fight!" - *Major General Frank E. Lowe, U.S. Army; Korea, 26 January 1952*

"We have two companies of Marines running rampant all over the northern half of this island, and three Army regiments pinned down in the southwestern corner, doing nothing. What the *hell* is going on?" - *General John W. Vessey Jr., U.S. Army, Chairman of the Joint Chiefs of Staff during the assault on Grenada, 1983*

"The raising of that flag on Suribachi means a Marine Corps for the next five hundred years." - *Secretary of the Navy James Forrestal*

"Here at Belleau Wood, the German commander was to risk all in a 'local dogfight.' And he had picked on the wrong people." - *Military historian S.L.A. Marshall*

"In a society that seems to have trouble transmitting healthy values, the Marines stand out as a successful institution that unabashedly teaches those values to the Beavises and Butt-heads of America." - *Thomas E. Ricks*

"Marines are mystical. They have magic." - *Author Tom Clancy*

"In one flash, as we charged across [the street] amid whistling incoming shots, I realized that they were *not* like me; they were Marines." - *Robert D. Kaplan*

"In my entire life, I have never seen anything like you. You're taking care of the mission. You're taking care of each other. You're acting like Marines. I won't make a long speech here. I just want you to know that if I had a son, I'd want him to be a Marine." - *General Tommy Franks, U.S. Army*

19

"The U.S. Marine Corps has a propaganda machine to rival Stalin's." - *President Harry S. Truman*

"The U.S. Marine Corps is more than a crack military machine. It is a fraternity bonded in blood." - *Clare Boothe Luce*

"The American Marines have it (pride) and benefit from it. They are tough, cocky, sure of themselves and their buddies. They can fight, and they know it." - *General Mark Clark, U.S. Army*

"By the time the Marines are through with them, the Japanese language will be spoken only in Hell!" - *Admiral William F. "Bull" Halsey*

"Marine basic training attempts to take a kid and turn him into a responsible, disciplined adult - in seventy training days. And it works." - *Dr. Pamela Grimm, M.D., Parris Island*

"I'd give a million dollars to be a Marine." - *Former heavyweight boxing champion Riddick Bowe, who failed to make it through boot camp*

"A million men cannot not take Tarawa in a hundred years." - *Japanese Rear Admiral Keiji Shibasaki (the Second Marine Division did it in three days)*

"The more Marines I have around me, the better I like it." - *General Mark Clark, U.S. Army*

"In the Army, shock troops are a small minority supported by a vast group of artisans, laborers, clerks, and organizers. In the Marines, there are practically nothing *but* shock troops." - *Combat correspondent John Lardner on Iwo Jima, 1945*

"Among the Americans who fought on Iwo Island, uncommon valor was a common virtue." - *Admiral Chester Nimitz*

"A *real* star... is the U.S. Marine in Baghdad who saw a little girl playing with a piece of unexploded ordnance on a street ... He pushed her aside and threw himself on it just as it exploded." - *Ben Stein, in his final column about "stars"*

"To say that his (Lt. William Deane Hawkins) conduct was worthy of the highest traditions of the Marine Corps is like saying the Empire State Building is moderately high." - *Robert Sherrod, then Editor of 'The Saturday Evening Post'*

"The story of Joe Foss's life is a story of human endeavor so great and so accomplished that it defies exaggeration." - *Senator John McCain*

"Where are the famous United States Marines hiding? The Marines are supposed to be the finest soldiers in the world, but no one has seen them yet?" - *Japanese radio propagandist as the 1st Marine Division was steaming toward Guadalcanal in 1942 (they would soon find out the answer to their question!)*

"He spelled out his message with extreme care amid the whistling snarl of Spanish bullets all round him, his back turned toward the enemy in apparent contempt for whatever they would do. He was magnificent." - *Stephen Crane, writing about Sergeant John Quick at Cuzco Wells*

"What shall I say of the gallantry with which these Marines fought? I cannot write of their splendid gallantry without tears coming to my eyes." - *Major General James Harbord, U.S. Army of the Marines at Belleau Wood*

"They have held the fort and kept Old Glory flying... they may yet be annihilated... but they have fought gallantly, and by their gallantry they have carried on in the finest tradition of their Corps." - *The New York Times, regarding the valiant defense of Wake Island*

"He contributed materially to the defeat, and virtually the annihilation, of a Japanese regiment." - *Chesty Puller on 'Manila' John Basilone*

"The Marines and the Navy have never shone more brightly than this morning." - *General Douglas MacArthur at Inchon, September 1950*

"The American First Marine Division has the highest combat effectiveness in the American armed forces. It seems not enough for our four divisions to surround and annihilate its two regiments. (You) should have one or two more divisions as a reserve force." - *Mao Zedong's orders to Chinese General Song Shilun*

"Retrieving wounded comrades from the field of fire is a Marine Corps tradition more sacred than life." - *Robert Pisor*

"The Marine Corps has just been called by the *New York Times*, 'The elite of this country.' I think it is the elite of the *world*." - *Admiral William "Bull" Halsey, U.S. Navy*

"There have been many Marines. And there have been many Marine marksmen. But there is only one Marine Sniper - Gunnery Sergeant Carlos N. Hathcock II. One Shot - One Kill." - *Inscription on a plaque presented to Gunnery Sergeant Carlos Hathcock (93 confirmed kills) at his retirement*

"Why in hell can't the Army do it if the Marines can? They are the same kind of men; why can't they be like Marines?" - *Army General John J. "Black Jack" Pershing, U.S. Army, on 12 February, 1918*

"Hue City (was) the sight of one of the most glorious chapters in Marine Corps history - in which the Marines killed 5,113 enemy troops while suffering 147 dead and 857 wounded... (but) the Marines never got proper credit for Hue, for it was ultimately overshadowed by My Lai." - *Robert D. Kaplan*

"...these Marines have the swagger, confidence, and hardness that must have been in Stonewall Jackson's Army of the Shenandoah. They remind me of the Coldstreams at Dunkerque." - *General Douglas MacArthur, U.S. Army*

"When my son left home he had no motivation, he was lazy, a slob, no pride, no self worth. That was the boy who got off the bus at Parris Island. The MAN that I met on Thursday for parent's day is AWESOME... I could never express my gratitude enough to the Marine Corps for what they have given my son." - *"Cybil," Mother of a Marine*

"They told (us) to open up the Embassy, or 'we'll blow you away.' And then they looked up and saw the Marines on the roof with these really big guns, and they said in Somali, 'Igaralli ahow,' which means "Excuse me, I didn't mean it, my mistake." - *Karen Aquilar, U.S. Embassy Mogadishu, Somalia, in 1991*

"Today, the world looks to America for leadership. And America looks to its Corps of Marines." - *President Ronald Reagan*

"A Marine should be sworn to the patient endurance of hardships, like the ancient knights; and it is not the least of these necessary hardships to have to serve with sailors." - *Field Marshal Bernard Law Montgomery*

"The man who will go where his colors go, without asking, who will fight a phantom foe in jungle and mountain range, without counting, and who will suffer and die in the midst of incredible hardship, without complaint, is still what he has always been, from Imperial Rome to sceptered Britain to democratic America. He is the stuff of which legions are made... he has been called United States Marine." - *Army Historian Colonel T. E. Fehrenbach*

"I feel shame, because it took my son's joining the Marine Corps to make me take notice of who is defending me." - *Author and 'Marine Dad' Frank Schaeffer*

"If you can read this, thank a teacher... If you are reading it in *English*, thank a Marine." - *From a bumper sticker*

"Cowards cut and run. Marines never do."
- *Representative Jean Schmidt (R-OH) on the floor of Congress, 2005*

"The Marines did a tremendous job. While most people were running *out* of the building, they were running *in*, despite the obvious danger." - *A senior State Department official, in the aftermath of our embassy in Nairobi being bombed by terrorists*

"Somewhere, somehow, he had taken the words honor, courage and commitment into his very soul and laid his life on the line daily for me and us... I realized I had rubbed shoulders with greatness in the flesh, and in the twinkling of an eye my life was forever changed. His name is Michael Mendez, a corporal in the USMC. We are a great nation. We know because the makings of it walked into my office that day." - *Ann Baker of Huntington Beach, California in a letter to the Orange County Register on June 30, 2002*

"What are our duties as Americans that our would-be-leaders ask of us? What sacrifices are we as Americans willing to make? I don't know. But the Marines know."
- *Columnist and former Marine Mark Shields in the Washington Post, October 1999*

"If you're looking for trouble, let me assure you these men will be glad to oblige. And if you've brought enough friends with you, you might even win this one. But, they'll be back. Tomorrow, maybe next week, but you can count on them coming back. With whatever and whoever it takes, they'll be back, and eventually you'll lose, and lose big." - *An Air Force Sergeant (who was a former Marine) warning a group of airmen who were antagonizing some Marines in Vietnam*

"I've never been so happy to see Marines in my life!" - *"Sandy," an ultra-liberal, military-hating State Department official who had just been rescued from a crossfire in the Congo*

"I receive over a 1,000 e-mails a week from service personnel. Most are rightfully grousing about bad leadership and conditions and lousy readiness. Few of these letters are from Marines. Dozens of times a week, young men ask me to recommend a branch of the service. My answer: If you want to be challenged and forge stronger values, better character and develop into a better person, join the Marines." - *Colonel David H. Hackworth, U.S. Army (Ret)*

"The children of fighter pilots tell different stories than other kids do... When we talk about the aviators who raised us and the Marines who loved us, we can look you in the eye and say 'you would not like to have been America's enemies when our fathers passed overhead.'"
- Pat Conroy in the eulogy for his father, Colonel Donald Conroy (aka 'The Great Santini')

"I wish I'd led a platoon of Marines in Vietnam. I would like to think I would have trained my troops well, and that the Viet Cong would have had their hands full if they entered a firefight with us... I understand now that I should have protested the war after my return from Vietnam, after I had done my duty for my country. I have come to a conclusion about my country that I knew then in my bones, but lacked the courage to act on: America is good enough to die for, even when she is wrong. - *Author and 'Son of Santini' Pat Conroy*

"Press bias is an ugly thing... nowhere is that bias more obvious than the establishment press choosing to identify criminals and other anti-social misfits by their former association with the U.S. Marine Corps, as in: 'Ex-Marine terrorizes shopping center.' Have you ever seen a story that began: 'Ex-draft-dodger convicted of bilking widows and orphans out of their life savings?'"
- *Columnist and former Marine Mark Shields in the Washington Post, October 1999*

"He died doing what he loved best, and that was being a Marine." - *Judy Childers, referring to her son 2nd Lieutenant Shane Childers, who was the first casualty in OIF*

"I think I understand Marines better now, but I'm not sure I can *explain* them." - *Correspondent Roger Roy in The Orlando Sentinel on April 27, 2003*

"I never knew many Marines who were only a 'little' dangerous. Most of them seemed to be a *lot* dangerous. That, I think, is the idea." - *former Air Force officer, Vietnam veteran and fighter pilot Toby Hughes*

"There is, for example, the unidentified Marine with his mouth set in a grimace from the bullet that passed through his knee. He tried to wave off comrades who eventually carried him to cover during the heaviest fighting for al-Azimiyah Palace in east Baghdad. While being carried he continued to fire his weapon at the enemy until his ammunition ran out." - *Reporter Richard Tomkins, who was embedded with Bravo 1/5 during OIF*

"The list of names of the men who did themselves proud, the Marines proud and their nation proud is too long to recite." - *Reporter Richard Tomkins, who was embedded with Bravo 1/5 during OIF*

"Dau-uy Dien! Dau-uy Dien!" (Captain Crazy! Captain Crazy!) - *South Vietnamese Marines witnessing the bravery of Captain John Ripley, USMC, at Dong Ha*

"So how to say thank you? How to say how much I love and respect them? Words can't do it. So like other reporters, I give them the smartest, snappiest salute I, as a civilian, can muster. God speed, Bravo 1/5, and Semper Fi." - *Reporter Richard Tomkins, who was embedded with Bravo 1/5 during OIF*

"This statue symbolizes the hopes and dreams of America, and the real purpose of our foreign policy. We realize that to retain freedom for ourselves, we must be concerned when people in other parts of the world may lose theirs." - *Vice President Richard M. Nixon on November 10, 1954, at the dedication of the Marine Corps War Memorial*

"The Americans who have been besieged in Peking desire to express their hearty appreciation of the courage, fidelity, and patriotism of the American Marines, to whom we so largely owe our salvation. By their bravery in holding an almost untenable position on the city wall in the face of overwhelming numbers, and in cooperating in driving the Chinese from a position of great strength, they made all foreigners in Peking their debtors, and have gained for themselves an honorable name among the heroes of their country." - *Arthur H. Smith and Charles E. Ewing, expressing a resolution unanimously adopted at the meeting of American missionaries in Peking on 18 August 1900*

"...there was something impressive about a lone Marine carrying out a ceremonial task which obviously meant very much to him and which, in its simplicity, made the might, the power and the glory of the United States of America stand forth in a way that a mighty wave of military aircraft, or the passage of a super-carrier, or a parade of 10,000 men could never have made manifest." – *Anonymous foreign diplomat, who had just witnessed a U.S. Marine retiring the colors at an American embassy abroad*

"His personal action was far beyond the call of duty, and saved the lives of his fellow Marines." - *Lieutenant Colonel Matthew Lopez, CO of Third Battalion, Seventh Marine Regiment, speaking about Corporal Jason Dunham in September of 2003*

"We're going to turn out all right, as long as men like Brian Chontosh wear our uniform. He is proof that we still make Marines like we used to." – *Anonymous*

"He was barefoot and his eyes were red as fire. His face was dirty black from gunfire and lack of sleep. His shirt sleeves were rolled up to his shoulders. He had a .45 tucked into the waistband of his trousers... I'll never forget him. He'll never be dead in my mind!" - *Nash Phillips, on John Basilone*

"Mrs. Virginia Calhoun received John's body, an American Flag, and the Navy Cross for John's heroism in battle. Somewhere his courage in the last moments of his life is recorded in an official military citation. Find it and read it if you wish. I don't have to." - *Edmund R. Driscoll Jr.*

"What I think the Marine Corps represents is a counterculture, but the Marines are rebels *with* a cause. With their emphasis on honor, courage, and commitment, they offer a powerful alternative to the loneliness and distrust that seems so widespread, especially among our youth." - *Thomas E. Ricks*

"When the other services talk about 'quality of life,' they are referring to housing, clubs and food. Marines are talking about better weapons, equipment and training."
"Ryan Swain is just twenty years old... but *Corporal Ryan Swain, USMC,* is a man of honor and courage. A man who is pledged to lay down his life for his home, his country. Together with young men and women from all parts of the United States of America, he is ready to defend us and our way of life." - *Cynthia Townley Ewer, mother of Corporal Ryan Swain*

"The worse conditions are, the better Marines seem to like it." - *Pamela Hess*

"As I was talking to one Marine, he told me his *greatest regret* was that he would no longer be able to serve beside his fellow Marines. The reason this brave young man could no longer serve was that he had lost both arms in combat." - *Chaplain Shane Dillman*

"His is the story of one dedicated individual who simple would not quit in the face of tremendous adversity, and who repeatedly demonstrated he had the courage, spirit, and self-determination to overcome his misfortune. Don Hamblen's extraordinary example of tenacity is personified in the phrase, 'one tough Marine.'" - *Major Bruce "Doc" Norton on Woody Hamblen, who overcame the loss of a leg to return to active duty and serve three tours in Vietnam*

"Not to take anything away from the U.S. Army – its soldiers have performed magnificently, and will no doubt continue to do so – but America's enemies have a particular fear of U.S. Marines." - *W. Thomas Smith Jr.*

"Marines are extremists. Wherever you have extremists, you've got some risks of total disconnection with society. And that's a little dangerous." - *Assistant Secretary of the Army Sara Lister, 1997*

"Your remarks were an affront to every Marine... you have impugned all who have served... and died for the very freedoms you enjoy." - *Senator Conrad Burns, in a letter to Assistant Secretary of the Army Sara Lister*

"Marines have distinguished themselves by their bravery, stubbornness, aggressive spirit, sacrifice, love of country, and loyalty to one another. They've done it for you and me, and this country we all love so dearly. And they asked for nothing more than the honor of being a United States Marine... *that's* why I like Marines!" - *Rear Admiral J. Stark, U.S. Navy, on 10 November 1995.*

"Although only twenty-two years old and 'only' an enlisted man, that young American (Dunham) exhibited a greater degree of loyalty, courage and decisiveness in a *moment* than many of us do in a *lifetime*." - *Master Sergeant Andy Bufalo, USMC (Ret)*

"(Captain) Smith did not have to order his Marines straight into the direction of the fire; it was a collective impulse - a phenomenon I would see again and again over the coming days. The idea that Marines are trained to break down doors, to seize beachheads and other territory, was an abstraction until I was there to experience it. Running *into* fire rather than seeking cover from it goes counter to every human survival instinct." - *Atlantic Monthly correspondent Robert D. Kaplan in his report "Five Days in Fallujah"*

"The law of nature is simple: survival of the fittest. And in the 21st century, heartbreaking as it is for me to admit, the forward-based and highly deployable U.S. Marine Corps is the fittest." – *Colonel David H. Hackworth, U. S. Army (Ret)*

"A ship without Marines is like a garment without buttons." - *Admiral David Porter, USN*

"I have been a dove all my life... (but) I don't want to hear anyone say *one word* against those Marines. Those Marines came down and saved us." - *College student Jeff Geller, who had just been rescued from Grenada in 1983*

"The Marines are the smallest of the U.S. military services. But if you were to gauge size merely by the number of bumper stickers on cars across America, the Marines would win hands-down as the largest." - *Kristine Kirby Webster*

"Two reporters were interviewing each other in Iraq, one embedded with the Army, the other with the Marines. The reporter with the Army noted that a sandstorm had blown down many of the soldiers' cots. The other reporter countered that the Marines did not have this problem - because they slept on the ground."

"Recently I was in an air terminal... most people there presented a pretty sloppy appearance – coats unbuttoned, ties loosened, etc. There was a Marine Corporal (in uniform) who was just the opposite. I spoke to the Marine, and pointed out the difference to him. I asked him why it was so? His answer was: 'The Marines don't do that'." - *Letter to Commandant Leonard F. Chapman from a distinguished friend*

"Wake Island became a watchword, a symbol, a heroic stand on the part of a handful of the glamorous leathernecks. Their courage eased some of the hurt and shame of Pearl Harbor." - *from the book 'Wake Island' by Duane Schultz*

"Marines have a cynical approach to war. They believe in three things: liberty, payday, and that when two Marines are together in a fight, one is being wasted. Being a minority group militarily, they are proud and sensitive in their dealings with other military organizations. A Marine's concept of a perfect battle is to have other Marines on the right and left flanks, Marine aircraft overhead, and Marine artillery and naval gunfire backing them up." - *Correspondent Ernie Pyle*

"We belong to a proud Corps. I have often said that pride is the high octane fuel of the Marine Corps. If you can't be proud, you can't be a Marine." - *Colonel John Ripley*

"The Army must return to the standard where every soldier truly is a rifleman first. The Marines still follow this rule, and when their support units in Iraq bumped into stay-behind fanatics they did what Marines have been doing well since 1775: killed the suckers and moved on!" - *Colonel David Hackworth, U.S. Army (Ret)*

"My only answer as to why the Marines get the toughest jobs is because the average Leatherneck is a much better fighter. He has far more guts, courage, and better officers... These boys out here have a pride in the Marine Corps, and will fight to the end no matter what the cost." - *2nd Lt. Richard C. Kennard, Peleliu, World War II*

"If I had one more division like this First Marine Division I could win this war." - *Army General Douglas McArthur in Korea, overheard and reported by Marine Staff Sergeant Bill Houghton*

"I will spend the rest of my hours on this earth announcing to the *world* (as I have in the past), how highly honored I am for having been privileged to serve alongside the *noblest* of warriors - those feisty U.S. MARINES! - *HM1 John Francis Richter USN (Ret), a veteran of Guadalcanal, Cape Gloucester, and Korea*

"I can't say enough about the two Marine divisions. If I use words like 'brilliant,' it would really be an under description of the absolutely superb job that they did in breaching the so-called 'impenetrable barrier.' It was a classic- absolutely classic- military breaching of a very very tough minefield, barbed wire, fire trenches-type barrier." - *General Norman Schwarzkopf, U. S. Army, February 1991*

"This was the first time that the Marines of the two nations had fought side by side since the defense of the Peking Legations in 1900. Let it be said that the admiration of all ranks of 41 Commando (of the Royal Marines) for their brothers in arms was and is unbounded. They fought like tigers, and their morale and esprit de corps is second to none." - *Lieutenant Colonel D.B. Drysdale, Commanding 41 Commando of the Royal Marines at the Chosin Reservoir, speaking about the 1st Marine Division*

"I can see the possibility we might be able to live without the Army, without a Navy, we might be able to live without the Air Force. But this country can *never* live without a Corps of lean, mean Marines." - *The Honorable David Packard, 10 November 1970*

"...The Marines have been the first to land - on embattled beaches throughout the world - we share the unfaltering confidence of all Americans that they will land again - and land hard." - *VAdm Herbert F. Leary, Commander Eastern Sea Frontier, 8 Nov. 1943*

"By the grace of God and a few Marines, MacArthur returned to the Philippines." - *Sign posted on the beach when General Douglas MacArthur "returned" to the Philippines*

"Freedom is not free, but the U.S. Marine Corps will pay most of your share." - *Ned Dolan*

The beginning and the end of the war for the Germans were the battles of the Marne – and with the name of Marne will always be associated that of the glorious American Marines... - *French Consul General Gaston Libert, 1918*

QUOTES BY MARINES

The Lore of the Corps

"It cannot be inherited, nor can it ever be purchased. You or no one alive can buy it for any price. It is impossible to rent, and it cannot be lent. You alone have earned it with your sweat, blood and tears. You own it forever - The title, 'United States Marine.'" - *An unknown Marine*

"My experience in the United States Marine Corps steered me onto the path of success. The Marine Corps instilled in me honor, courage and commitment - core values that have sustained me through thick and thin." - *Senator Zell Miller (former sergeant, USMC)*

"Casualties: many, Percentage of dead: not known, Combat efficiency: we are winning." - *Colonel David M. Shoup, Tarawa, 21 November 1943*

"I was a PFC in the Marine Corps, so when I started playing officers (in the movies) I had a good opinion as to how they should be portrayed – from the bias of an enlisted man's viewpoint." - *Actor Lee Marvin*

"A battalion commander didn't need a staff, he got out in front of his battalion and he *led* it." - *Chesty Puller*

"...The medals still represented the dignity and the caliber of my service and of those with whom I served... I could no more discard them than I could repudiate my country, my Marine Corps or my fellow veterans." - *Lewis B. Puller Jr. in his Pulitzer Prize-winning book 'Fortunate Son'*

"I'd rather be a Marine Private than a civilian executive." - *Major H.G. "Dunk" Duncan*

"I think when people begin to understand what happened in World War II they have a leg up on knowing who we are as a people, what we are, and how strong we can be if we need to be." - *Medal of Honor recipient Bill Barber*

"This is a time for all Americans to reflect on what it means to be an American. We have gone across the seas in years past to fight in the defense of the freedoms we hold so dear, but this time the battlefield is closer to home - too close." - *Medal of Honor recipient Colonel Harvey C. "Barney" Barnum USMC*

"I liked being in the Marines. They gave me discipline I could live with... sure I was pretty wild – but I had a lot of rough edges knocked off." - *Actor Steve McQueen*

"They don't give a damn *who* they shoot, do they, Chaplain?" - *General Lemuel C. Shepherd, while visiting Chaplain Connie Griffin, who had just been wounded during the Korean War*

"He was just a kid, as was I. He confided to me that he had never even kissed a girl before... unfortunately, he never got the chance. I think his mother would be happy to know that only she and God ever knew the tenderness of his kiss." - *A friend of PFC Bruce E. Cunningham, KIA in Vietnam*

"The only thing bigger than a Marine's mouth is his heart." - *Major H.G. "Dunk" Duncan*

"I had the unpleasant opportunity to view the new movie 'Fahrenheit 9/11' by Michael Moore last night. I have never been so offended in my life." - *Corporal W.M. Howard II, Iraq*

"Those of us who have had the privilege of serving in the Marine Corps value our experience as among the most precious of our lives. The fellowship of shared hardships and dangers in a worthy cause creates a close bond of comradeship. It is the basic reason for the cohesiveness of Marines and for the pride we have in our Corps and our loyalty to each other." - *Senator and Former Marine Paul H. Douglas*

"He insisted on giving his life so that forty of his fellow Marines might live and triumph. He had freely chosen loyalty above life." - *First Lieutenant Michael Stick, speaking of Corporal Larry Maxam, KIA RVN 1968*

"Whatever else we are or may become for the rest of our lives, if you have once been a Marine, you are always a Marine." - *Author James Brady*

"If I had to rank the Leadership Traits, I'd have to place 'integrity' at the top." - *Major H.G. "Dunk" Duncan*

"I've got some bad news, and some good news. The bad news is we will be filling sandbags until the next Japanese attack. The good news is, we have plenty of sand." - *Marine Gunnery Sergeant on Wake Island, 1941*

"God favors the bold and the strong of heart." - *General A.A. Vandegrift before D-Day at Guadalcanal*

"He contributed materially to the defeat, and virtually the annihilation, of a Japanese regiment." - *Chesty Puller on 'Manila' John Basilone*

"We have lost many friends, and now it is time for the **enemy** to lose some." - *John Tanney at Khe Sahn in April of 1968*

"The warrior has come center stage once again, and it is time for the tender-hearted to take a seat and be quiet. The warrior will ensure that they, the talkers, retain all of their rights, to include letting the warrior do the tough, ugly work." - *Colonel Wesley Fox on fighting the 'War on Terrorism'*

"We signed up knowing the risk. Those innocent people in New York didn't go to work thinking there was any kind of risk." - *Private Mike Armendariz-Clark, USMC September 20, 2001*

"We fought for each other, and to uphold the honor of the Corps." - *Captain Angus Deming, USMC*

"Old breed? New breed? There's not a damn bit of difference so long as it's the *Marine* breed!" - *Lieutenant General Lewis B. Puller*

"The bended knee is not a tradition of our Corps." - *General Alexander A. Vandergrift, USMC to the Senate Naval Affairs Committee, 1946*

"You'll never get a Purple Heart hiding in a foxhole! Follow me!" - *Captain Henry P. Crowe, USMC on Guadalcanal, 13 January 1943*

"Come on, you sons of bitches! Do you want to live forever?" - *GySgt Daniel J. "Dan" Daly as he led the 5th Marines' attack into Belleau Wood, 6 June 1918*

"Don't you forget that you're First Marines! Not all the communists in Hell can overrun you!" - *Colonel Lewis B. "Chesty" Puller, rallying his First Marine Regiment near the Chosin Reservoir*

"I have only two men out of my company and twenty out of some other company. We need support, but it is almost suicide to try to get it here as we are swept by machine gun fire and a constant barrage is on us. I have no one on my left, and only a few on my right. I will hold." - *First Lieutenant (and future Commandant) Clifton B. Cates, USMC in Belleau Wood, on 19 July 1918*

"I love the Corps for those intangible possessions that cannot be issued: pride, honor, integrity, and being able to carry on the traditions for generations of warriors past." - *Corporal Jeff Sornij, USMC; in Navy Times, November 1994*

"The enemy is to the left of us, the enemy is to the right of us, they're in front of us, and they're behind us. The poor bastards won't get away this time!" - *"Chesty" Puller*

"For over 221 years our Corps has done two things for this great Nation. We make Marines, and we win battles." - *General Charles C. Krulak USMC May, 1997*

"The thing I'm most proud of is that I was a Marine Corps fighter pilot." - *Baseball legend Ted Williams*

"Some people *wave* the flag, but *waive* what it stands for – and none of them are Marines!" - *Master Sergeant Andy Bufalo, USMC (Ret)*

"Semper Fidelis works both ways – we are always faithful to the Corps, and the Corps remains faithful to us." - *Master Sergeant Andy Bufalo, USMC (Ret)*

"It is the soldier, not the reporter who has given us freedom of the press. It is the soldier, not the poet, who has given us freedom of speech. It is the soldier, not the campus organizer, who gives us freedom to demonstrate. It is the soldier who salutes the flag, who serves beneath the flag, and whose coffin is draped by the flag, who allows the protester to burn the flag." - *Father Dennis O'Brien, Former Sergeant, USMC*

"Gone to Florida to fight the Indians. Will be back when the war is over." - *Colonel Commandant Archibald Henderson, USMC in a note pinned to his office door, 1836*

"All who now wear, or have ever worn, the eagle, globe and anchor share a common bond." - *Senator and former Marine Charles Robb*

"The mere association of the word 'Marine' with a crisis is an automatic source of confidence to America, and is encouragement to all." - *Colonel "Irish" Egan USMC (Ret)*

"It is friendship, and something beyond friendship, that binds the Marine Corps together." - *Secretary of State Donald Regan*

"He died a Marine, holding his position, facing the enemy, rifle in hand. And I don't much care what he had written on his helmet." - *Lieutenant Colonel Steve Richmond, USMC*

"You've done your job, Mom. Now it is *my* turn to protect *you*." - *Sergeant Byron Norwood USM, Iraq*

"We are at last standing up against a modern day Hitler and using our fist. If we had done something positive the first time the Trade Center was bombed, we would have six thousand more citizens today." - *Medal of Honor recipient Colonel Wesley Fox, USMC*

"Those who are wringing their hands and shouting so loudly for 'heads to roll' over [the Iraq prison abuse] seem to have conveniently overlooked the fact that someone's head *has* rolled - that of another innocent American brutally murdered by terrorists. Why is it that there's more indignation over a photo of a prisoner with underwear on his head, than over the video of a young American with no head at all?" - *Senator and former Marine Zell Miller*

"When a Marine in Vietnam is wounded, surrounded, hungry, low on ammunition or water, he looks to the sky. He knows the choppers are coming..." - *General Leonard F. Chapman, Commandant of the Marine Corps*

"Medevac? What do you mean, medevac? It's just a scratch. Who do you think I am, John Kerry?" - *Uttered by a seriously wounded Marine during a firefight in Fallujah*

"I almost feel pity for the poor stupid thugs in Fallujah who had dared tangle with the Marines. 'You jerks haven't got a chance. Just call Dr. Kevorkian and get it over with.'" - *State Department employee*

"We're Marines! We took Iwo Jima! Baghdad ain't shit!" - *General Kelly, First Marines, on proceeding to Baghdad*

"We must all remember that leaders like General Mattis and the men he commands are the rarest commodities that a protected society like ours can produce." - *Major General Robert H. Scales, U.S. Army*

"Did you hear what the Marine officer in Haiti who - when asked on Sunday what he knew about the Haitian gunman who was part of the shooting into the crowd on Saturday – said?: 'I only know two things about him; he shot at my Marines... and he's dead.'" - *Lieutenant General Robert M. Shea, USMC*

"The young captain really got to me. Many thoughts of so long ago. In my opinion, these guys are better than we were. That's the way it should be. Otherwise, we did not do our job." - *Major General Jarvis Lynch, USMC*

"I didn't know the Marines who died, but I miss them just the same." - *Former Marine Kevin C. Jones, after hearing a news report about the crash of a Marine Corps CH-53 helicopter*

"I'd rather be an outstanding sergeant than just another officer." - *Dan Daly*

"I am sorry that the last seven times we Americans took up arms and sacrificed the blood of our youth, it was in the defense of Muslims." - *Attributed to Lieutenant General Chuck Pittman, USMC (Ret)*

"It must be puzzling to our enemies as to how the bravery of the warriors they face in combat can be offset by the cowardly and self-serving behavior those far from harm's way publicly display at every opportunity." - *Captain Dave St. John, USMCR*

"Wherever I go, everyone is a little bit safer because I am there. Wherever I am, anyone in need has a friend. Whenever I return home, everyone is happy I am there." - *Bob Humphreys' "Warrior's Creed"*

"It is respectfully requested that my present assignment to a combat unit be extended until the downfall of the Japanese government." – *LtCol Chesty Puller, to the Commandant of the Marine Corps, in April of 1943*

"If he wants to decorate me, he'll have to come up here." - *Chesty Puller, on hearing that General MacArthur had come ashore at Inchon and wanted to give him a medal.*

"Nothing makes this Marine madder than someone calling American troops occupiers, rather than liberators." - *Senator (and former Marine) Zell Miller*

"This is a man who wants to be the commander in chief of our U.S. armed forces? Armed with what? Spitballs?" - *Senator (and former Marine) Zell Miller*

"I wish we lived in the day when you could challenge a person to a duel!" - *Senator (and former Marine) Zell Miller*

"Our Country won't go on forever, if we stay as soft as we are now. There won't be any AMERICA because some foreign soldiery will invade us and take our women and breed a hardier race!" - *"Chesty" Puller*

"Where does the bayonet go?" - *Chesty Puller's question the first time he was shown a flame thrower*

"Send us more Japs!" - *Legendary response from Major James Devereaux, the Marine Commander on Wake Island, when asked what he needed shortly before the island fell to the Japanese in December of 1941*

"For the last ten years, we Americans have been hit numerous times by terrorists with the resulting loss of many lives. We knew who were behind the acts and we negotiated, we talked. Our good intentions were for nothing; we are seen as ineffective, as paper tigers, so we are slapped harder. Some people who share our world understand and respect only the fist, not words."
- *Colonel Wesley Fox, USMC (Ret)*

"The road to hell is paved with the bleached bones of leaders who forgot to put out local security." - *Chesty Puller*

"You can't beat the United States Marine Corps. If you think you can, I'll thump you right now!" - *Master Sergeant Franklin D. Jones, USMC*

"The coming battle of Fallujah will be no different than the historic fights at Inchon in Korea, the flag-raising victory at Iwo Jima, or the bloody assault to dislodge North Vietnamese from the ancient citadel of Hue. You're all in the process of making history. This is another Hue city in the making. I have no doubt, if we do get the word, that each and every one of you is going to do what you have always done - kick some butt."
- *Sergeant Major Carlton W. Kent*

"When the time comes to lay down my life for my country, I do not cower from this responsibility. I welcome it." - *Corporal Aaron M. Gilbert, U.S. Marine Corps*

"The Corps is not a finishing school. It is not a game. It's a way of life – and it's basic purpose is to maintain the fact that a combat Marine is the best fighting soldier in the world." - *Legendary film director and former Marine Sam Peckinpah, in a letter to his son after the latter joined the Marine Corps*

"It is for me a touchstone of the Marine Corps' fatal glamour that there is no ex-Marine of my acquaintance, regardless of what direction he may have taken spiritually and politically after those callow gung-ho days, who does not view the training as a crucible out of which he emerged in some way more resilient, simply braver and better for the wear." - *Former Marine and Pulitzer Prize-winning author William Styron*

"If you really want to be the absolute best, you go into the Marine Corps. There's a tremendous psychic energy in the Marines, there always has been. It was one of the greatest moments of my life when I was commissioned as a Marine." - *Former Secretary of the Navy and bestselling author James Webb*

"(Marine Corps training) for the most part defined me and set me on a course for a disciplined life." - *Former Marine Montel Williams*

"I know what it is to become brothers with men you never would have met in the civilian world, and to remember them for years after they're gone." - *Former Marine Kevin C. Jones*

"I am no politician, and I am no expert on war, but I love my country, and my Marine Corps." - *Lance Corporal John McConnell, USMC*

"My Marine Corps experience has served me well. Everyone has heard about the pride of the Marines. Through training, both physical and psychological, we were given a very positive feeling about our capabilities. A very high esteem, something more parents should give their children." - *Former Marine Bob Keeshan (Captain Kangaroo)*

"(My Marine Corps service) was the first time I had a real sense of pride about myself, a sense of belonging to a group that's special. To this day, I'm proud of being a Marine." - *Actor and former Marine Harvey Keitel*

"I firmly believe that becoming a Marine was the defining experience of my life. Any success I have achieved, I feel I owe in no small measure to the values and principles I learned in the Marine Corps." - *Actor and former Marine Joe Lisi (Lt. Swersky on TV's 'Third Watch')*

"My Marine Corps experience means a great deal to me in many ways. The camaraderie, discipline and tenacity I learned helped me face some awful situations in my life." - *Actor and former Marine Gerald O'Loughlin (TV's 'The Rookies')*

"Every nation fears us." - *Master Sergeant Vincent Yates, USMC*

"This will be a battle between good and evil... It will be an honor to fight for God, country and the good of mankind." - *Lance Corporal Thomas C. Macedo, 20 Sept 2001*

"I watched Marines die face down in the mud protecting freedom." - *Lieutenant Colonel Oliver North*

"I did not pick these men. They were delivered by fate and the U.S. Marine Corps. But I know them in a way that I know no other men. I have never given anyone such trust. They were willing to guard something more precious than my life. They would have carried my reputation, the memory of me." - *Michael Norman, USMC*

"No Better Friend, No Worse Enemy." - *Motto of the First Marine Division in Iraq*

"I miss my family, my friends and my country, but right now there is nowhere else I'd rather be. I am a United States Marine." - *Major Glen G. Butler, USMC in Iraq*

"We destroyed the enemy like only Marines can... Previous to yesterday the terrorists thought that we were soft enough to challenge. As of tonight the message is loud and clear that the Marines will not be beaten. It will be a cold day in Hell before we are taken for granted again." - *Paul Kennedy, 2/4, Iraq*

"It's easy to call one who loves war mad, but the Marine who does not yearn to go to a raging battle is mere image and nothing more." - *Major H.G. "Dunk" Duncan*

"How does getting a twenty million dollar plane shot out from under him make (Air Force Captain Scott) O'Grady a hero? The *real* heroes were the Marines who went in and rescued him!" - *Tampa news anchor (and former Marine) Bob Hite*

"I could use some more ammunition, Sir." - *Marine Private from Battalion Landing Team 2/4 responding to General Tommy Franks, who had asked if there was anything he needed*

"The common thread which binds us together is a Marine's love of country, desire to protect our democracy, and belief in liberating the oppressed. Most of us join this gun club, at least in part, because we believe in what our country stands for. Every one of us is an instrument of democracy, and weapon for freedom." - *Master Sergeant Andy Bufalo, USMC (Ret)*

"One of the *worst* things the Army ever did was issue Black Berets for wear by all soldiers. In typical Army fashion they tried to boost morale and aid the recruiting effort by giving out a trinket to the rank and file, but when they did that it became *just another hat*. It was also an insult to the Rangers who had previously worn it. They are the closest thing to Marines the Army has, and such fine soldiers deserve better than that."
- *Master Sergeant Andy Bufalo, USMC (Ret)*

"What are our duties as Americans that our would-be-leaders ask of us? What sacrifices are we as Americans willing to make? I don't know. But the Marines know."
- *Columnist and former Marine Mark Shields in The Washington Post, October 1999*

"If you can believe it, the Army and Air Force actually award a ribbon for completing basic training. The Marine Corps, with a far more demanding boot camp, simply awards the right to be called 'Marine.' The next thing you know, they will issue every soldier a beret..."
- *Master Sergeant Andy Bufalo, USMC (Ret)*

"If you have one Marine without a field jacket and you are wearing one, you aren't much of a leader." - *Major H.G. "Dunk" Duncan*

"One of the things which inspires the Marines of today to go forth and do great and heroic things is the legacy of those who have gone before. No Marine wants to be the one to bring discredit upon the Corps, or sully the names of Daly and Butler and Puller." - *Master Sergeant Andy Bufalo, USMC (Ret)*

"Press bias is an ugly thing... nowhere is that bias more obvious than the establishment press choosing to identify criminals and other anti-social misfits by their former association with the U.S. Marine Corps, as in: 'Ex-Marine terrorizes shopping center.' Have you ever seen a story that began: 'Ex-draft-dodger convicted of bilking widows and orphans out of their life savings?'"
- *Columnist and former Marine Mark Shields in The Washington Post, October 1999*

"The best test of bearing is being seen in a shower room by a total stranger who calls you 'Sir'" - *Major H.G. "Dunk" Duncan*

"We want you to join the Marine Corps for one reason and for one reason only - because you want to be a Marine." - *Captain Jeff Sammons, USMC*

"If you have ever heard that song (the Marines' Hymn) played on the (bag)pipes you know the sound is almost spiritual." - *Master Sergeant Andy Bufalo, USMC (Ret)*

"The Marine Corps takes most everything to an extreme, and cleaning the barracks is no exception." - *Master Sergeant Andy Bufalo, USMC (Ret)*

"Anyone who has not seen it at least once is missing out on one of the great thrills that come with being a Marine. If you can't get motivated watching the Silent Drill Team you have to be crazy, or dead." - *Master Sergeant Andy Bufalo, USMC (Ret)*

"We didn't even have a map of Korea. Not zip. We just headed toward the sound of artillery firing along the Naktong River. They told us to keep the North Koreans on their side of the Naktong. Air power hadn't been a factor until we got there that day. I radioed to Bill Lundin - I was his wingman. 'There they are. Let's go get'em.' So we did." - *Colonel Donald Conroy*

"Dad gave 32 years of his life to the Marine Corps, (and) when he really, really needed the Corps, they were there for him." - *Former Marine Stephen Ripley, son of Colonel John Ripley*

"If you have never attended a Mess Night, or worse yet have never *heard* of such an occasion, you are missing out on one of the finest traditions the Marine Corps has to offer. It is an evening of camaraderie that, when properly run, can evoke many emotions in even the hardest of men." - *Master Sergeant Andy Bufalo, USMC (Ret)*

"I'm so proud to be called an American!" - *Lance Corporal John B. Santamaria, who had just taken the oath to become an American citizen after being wounded in Iraq*

"Semper Fi" - *Scrawled on a note pad by Lance Corporal Jeffery Nashton while on life support in the wake of the Beirut bombing, after blindly feeling the four stars of General P.X. Kelly*

"Cut, torn, bruised and dilapidated, they had marched without murmur for twenty-nine days." - *Major L. W. T. Waller, writing about the march across Samar*

"I never saw Gunny Tchaikovsky again after that terrible morning in early November. He was killed about an hour after he carried Barnes out of harm's way while saving *another* one of his precious Marines from an almost certain death. The date was 10 November 1966, my first Marine Corps Birthday in the Corps... (but) I know where Gunnery Sergeant Tchaikovsky is today. Rest assured, he is taking care of those beloved Marines who have been called back to guard the pearly gates!"
- *Harrison Greene*

"I remember one recruiting pamphlet which described the Marine Corps as 'the cold hard fist of American sea power thrust ashore.' I didn't really understand it sitting in my recruiter's office, but sitting on an amphibious ship off the coast of Beirut with a loaded rifle in my hands its meaning became clear." - *Master Sergeant Andy Bufalo, USMC (Ret)*

"Once you prove yourself to us you have a responsibility to honor our emblem and to maintain our traditions so that you are not the first to lose a battle or the first to dishonor those who have gone before and given all they had to make the name 'Marine' stand for something."
- *Retired Marine Corps Major William J. Peters*

"My friends and my Marines are still there, still fighting... any Marine in their right mind would want to be right there with them. All I've really lost is about ten degrees of peripheral vision, and I'll be OK without that. I'm ready to be with my Marines again." - *Gunnery Sergeant Nick Popaditch, who lost an eye fighting in Iraq*

"One of the things which sets a Marine apart from the average Joe Blow is the ability to tolerate unpleasant situations while in the pursuit of an objective. This characteristic has enabled wounded Marines to take hills and establish beachheads for over two centuries, and it is part of the Marine persona even during peacetime. When a good Marine sets his sights on a goal or is assigned a task he rarely lets anything stand in his way, even if it causes him to suffer." - *Master Sergeant Andy Bufalo, USMC (Ret)*

"A Marine's grave is sacred ground, no matter where it may be." - *Major H.G. "Dunk" Duncan*

"A study a few years back found that airmen leaving the military make the transition to civilian life almost seamlessly, soldiers are able to do so in a matter of weeks, and sailors lost the last vestiges of their military service within a year. The same study found that the vast majority of Marines *never* completely divest themselves of the traits and characteristics of the Corps. Ever notice how Marine Corps bumper stickers outnumber those of the other services by a huge margin, even though we are the smallest service? It's a small thing, but it says a lot. Once a Marine, always a Marine." - *Master Sergeant Andy Bufalo, USMC (Ret)*

"STAND, GENTLEMEN, HE SERVED ON SAMAR!"
- For many years after the march across Samar officers and men of the Marine Corps paid this traditional tribute to the indomitable courage of those Marines by rising in their presence with these words of homage

"I talked to a State Department type who had been trapped in the U.S. Embassy in Kuwait during Iraq's invasion. He had tears in his eyes as he spoke of the hardships imposed by the Iraqis and the guts and strength of the Marine Security Guards. He marveled at their arrogance in the face of overwhelming Iraqi troops... and (the Marines) always, always told them, 'You are with Marines. You are safe. Nothing will happen to you.'" - *Retired Marine Corps Major William J. Peters*

"Retirement is a difficult thing for many of us to accept after spending our lives in the Corps, but like death it is a fact of life. After all, even Chesty Puller had to retire." - *Master Sergeant Andy Bufalo, USMC (Ret)*

"We had a strong bond with our High School sports teammates, and some of those can last a lifetime. Most don't. But where else can you find the camaraderie we have with a million or more living Marines?" - *John Wintersteen*

"One of the things that makes the Marine Corps different (and better) is we know our history. Ask *any* Marine where the Corps was founded, who the first Commandant was, or the year of our birth, and he will tell you 'Tun Tavern, Captain Samuel Nicholas and 1775' without hesitation. That is because we use our history as a foundation upon which the Marines of each succeeding generation build." - *Master Sergeant Andy Bufalo, USMC*

"Retreat? Hell, we just got here!" - *Captain Lloyd Williams*

"If every American went through Marine Corps boot camp many of the social problems in our society would be eliminated." - *Master Sergeant Andy Bufalo, USMC*

"One of the first things to impress me about the Marine Corps was the way my Drill Instructors referred to the black recruits in my platoon as "dark green Marines." They said *all* Marines were green, just in different shades, and that we all bleed the same color – red."
- Master Sergeant Andy Bufalo, USMC (Ret)

"Marines are 'Soldiers of the Sea,' and it is right and proper that conversation be sprinkled with nautical expressions." - *Colonel James W. Hammond Jr., USMC (Ret)*

"There are Army officers and soldiers, Navy officers and sailors, Air Force officers and airmen, but we are *all* Marines. That is why Marine is always written with a capital 'M.'" - *Colonel James W. Hammond Jr., USMC*

"It is gratifying when some stranger at a cocktail party says, 'You sound like you're a Marine.'" - *Colonel James W. Hammond Jr., USMC (Ret)*

"The Spartans were arguably the greatest warriors of their time, just as Marines are the greatest of ours."
- Master Sergeant Andy Bufalo, USMC (Ret)

"Always, always, remember that no one can take your integrity from you. You and *only* you can give it away!"
- General Charles Krulak, Commandant of the Marine Corps

"Honey, I could come home right now, but I'm a Marine. And I have responsibilities. I'm a squad leader, and my Marines need me. And I'm going to go back." - *Corporal Timothy C. Tardif in a phone call to his wife from Landstuhl Hospital in Germany. He had been wounded twice, but chose to return to Iraq rather than be medevaced to the States*

"When I presented the flag to the mother, wife, or father (of a fallen Marine), I always said, "All Marines share in your grief." I had been instructed to say, "On behalf of a grateful nation," (but) I didn't think the nation was grateful, so I didn't say that." - *Lieutenant Colonel George Goodson*

"Sometimes it's hard for some Marines, especially those in support roles, to remember that we are all part of the same team. Force Recon and the infantry may be out at the 'tip of the spear,' but without someone to feed, clothe, and supply them they would all be hungry, naked, and unarmed (although, no doubt, still highly motivated!)." - *Master Sergeant Andy Bufalo, USMC (Ret)*

"The Marine Corps has a tested tradition; it will never leave alone on the field of combat one of its fighting men. It will go to fantastic lengths and commit to battle scores of men to aid and protect a few." - *Captain Francis J. West in 'Howard's Hill'*

"I want to make sure everyone makes it home alive. I want to be sure you go home to your wife alive." - *Jason Dunham on planning to extend his enlistment and stay in Iraq (he later sacrificed his life to save his brother Marines)*

"I sometimes wonder how my mom would have handled losing me in combat. I always made it a point to remind her that I loved the Corps and what it stood for, because I have always believed it lightens the load somewhat if your parents know you are doing something in which you strongly believe." - *Master Sergeant Andy Bufalo, USMC (Ret)*

"In the Marine Corps we have a special place in our hearts for our chaplains – and that includes those Marines who are not 'believers.' They are there for us when the going gets the roughest, and in the back of our minds we know a chaplain may well be the last person we see on this earth." - *Master Sergeant Andy Bufalo, USMC (Ret)*

"I think the truth of the matter is most of the so-called 'conscientious objectors' out there don't so much object to the idea of killing another human being, as they do to putting themselves in a situation where they *themselves* could get killed. Why not just be honest and say 'I'm scared,' instead of pretending to have lofty ideals?" - *Master Sergeant Andy Bufalo, USMC (Ret)*

"I like it that Marines say the term 'politically correct' with nothing but pure disdain." - *Colonel James M. Lowe, USMC*

"'Not As Lean, Not As Mean, Still A Marine,' is a nice way of saying that while each of us is truly 'once a Marine, always a Marine,' we also have to pass the torch on to the 'new breed' at some point. - *Master Sergeant Andy Bufalo, USMC (Ret)*

"Setting an example is the most difficult thing about leading men in combat... you're the one they're looking at for leadership. You need to be one step ahead, and always have them on your mind. Somebody is watching everything you're doing: all of your decisions, your emotions and your actions." - *Lieutenant George J. Flynn*

"The young Marines of today are already building upon the legacy which has been passed to them... so all of you old salts can rest easy – our beloved Corps is in good hands!" - *Master Sergeant Andy Bufalo, USMC (Ret)*

"The Leadership Principles are a cornerstone of our Marine Corps' ethos, but if we don't take the time to really *understand* each of them they are nothing more than a list of fourteen words." - *Master Sergeant Andy Bufalo, USMC (Ret)*

"Others say they want to be like us, but don't have what it takes in the "pain-gain-pride" department to make it happen." - *Colonel James M. Lowe, USMC*

"I will never forget my recruiter telling me 'I don't think you have what it takes to be a Marine,' while the other services were offering me the moon to sign on the dotted line." - *Master Sergeant Andy Bufalo, USMC (Ret)*

"I'd like to do it all over again. The whole thing. And more than that – more than anything – I'd like to see once again the face of every Marine I've ever served with." - *Chesty Puller, reminiscing about his career*

"During Operation Iraqi Freedom the Marines got the tough slogging on the way to Baghdad, much the same way they got the tough assignments from MacArthur during the Korean War – and that's the way it should be. Army generals may be jealous, and even resentful, of the Marine Corps, but they rarely fail to use us to good advantage when given the opportunity." - *Master Sergeant Andy Bufalo, USMC (Ret)*

"Marines know the difference between 'chicken salad' and 'chicken shit,' and aren't afraid to call either what it is!" - *Colonel James M. Lowe USMC*

"There is a famous photograph of (Ted) Williams standing next to a recruiting poster bearing his likeness, and what he did in that picture speaks volumes about his pride in being a Marine. The words on the poster say 'He Was A Marine,' and Williams is shown holding a hand-lettered card up to the poster that said, simply, 'IS.' After all, 'once a Marine, always a Marine.'" - *Master Sergeant Andy Bufalo, USMC (Ret)*

"'Ooh-rah' comes from the places in our hearts that only Marines understand. It is conceived in sweat, nurtured with drill. It is raw determination and gut-wrenching courage in the face of adversity. It is a concern for fellow Marines embodied by selfless acts of heroism. It cannot be administrated. It is not planned and put into action. It cannot be manufactured. Ooh-rah must be purchased. Ooh-rah is Marine." - *Gunnery Sergeant Glenn Holloway*

"Anyone who disrespects one of our beloved Navy Corpsmen in the presence of a Marine is signing his own death warrant!" - *Master Sergeant Andy Bufalo, USMC*

"The Army doesn't understand when you give something away cheaply it loses its value, as well as its meaning. You will not have to look any farther than Jessica Lynch being awarded the Bronze Star to know that is true. I am beginning to believe it is harder to get a Marine Corps Good Conduct Medal than an Army Bronze Star." - *Master Sergeant Andy Bufalo, USMC (Ret)*

"Don't worry if you are ready for the task of war. Because no sane man is ever ready. There is only one thing that makes a good warrior, and that is a man who cares for his fellow man. That is why the Marines do so well at making war. We respect each other. We'd rather die than to let down our comrades." - *General A. A. Vandegrift USMC*

"The only people who don't appreciate freedom are those who have been given it, free of charge." - *Lance Corporal T.M. Barmmer, who was KIA on January 30, 1968*

"I'd follow him to hell – and it looks like I'm going to have to." - *Marine officer in Korea, referring to Chesty Puller*

"Marines do things on a daily basis that would be inconceivable to a yuppie, and for us it's just another day at the office." - *Master Sergeant Andy Bufalo, USMC (Ret)*

"To serve under Chesty was to have a good chance to die... and yet enlisted Marines, who are not given to the adulation of their generals, fought for the chance to follow him." - *Ambassador Smith Hempstone, who had served with Chesty Puller in the 1st Marine Division during the Korean War*

"Something hard won is not easily relinquished."
- *Master Sergeant Andy Bufalo, USMC (Ret)*

 "Ever since the world began there have been meat-eaters and grass-eaters, those who would fight and those who would rather talk." - *Ambassador and former Marine Smith Hempstone*

"Later in my career I took to giving out dictionaries to some of my Marines (because I am a stickler for proper spelling and grammar), but before I did so I blacked out words like 'quit' and 'fail' because such words have no place in the vocabulary of a United States Marine."
- *Master Sergeant Andy Bufalo, USMC (Ret)*

"Doing a stateside tour is tougher than fighting Japs."
- *'Manila' John Basilone*

"I came here to kill Japs, not to be evacuated." - *First Lieutenant William Deane Hawkins after being wounded*

"Marines will low-crawl through a thousand miles of barbed wire and broken glass to help a brother Marine or a member of his family - even when they have never met." – *Master Sergeant Andy Bufalo, USMC (Ret)*

"I served 23 years in the United States Marine Corps. I served through two wars. I flew 149 combat missions. My plane was hit by antiaircraft fire on twelve different occasions... I *have* held a job, Howard! - what about you?" - *Senator John Glenn's reply to Howard Metzenbaum, a wealthy, self-made millionaire who had accused Glenn, as a 'lifetime government employee,' of never having held a job.*

"It seems like I spent my entire career in the Marine Corps waiting for something to end – be it a night's duty, a week in the field, a month aboard ship, or a year in Okinawa." - *Master Sergeant Andy Bufalo, USMC (Ret)*

"Stop a soldier on the street and ask him to name a battle of World War One. Pick a sailor at random to describe the epic fight of the Bon Homme Richard. Everyone has heard of McGuire Air Force Base, so ask any airman who Major Thomas B. McGuire was, and why he is so commemorated. I am not carping, and there is no sneer in this criticism. All of the services have glorious traditions, but no one teaches the young soldier, sailor, or airman what his uniform means and why he should be proud to wear it. But ask a Marine about World War One, and you will hear of the wheat field at Belleau Wood, and the courage of the Fourth Marine Brigade!" - *Author Unknown (but he was obviously a Marine!)*

"Sara Lister (who had called Marines 'extremists') had about as much business serving in the Department of Defense as I would have designing ladies evening wear, and her appointment made about as much sense as making a ballerina the linebackers coach for the Green Bay Packers." - *Master Sergeant Andy Bufalo, USMC (Ret)*

"We Marines have always prided ourselves on being squared away, positive role models. We have the Silent Drill Platoon. We spit shine our boots. We field day our barracks until you can eat off the deck, and stand wall locker inspections where one 'Irish pennant' is cause for failure. But the thing we admire above all else is personal heroism." - *Master Sergeant Andy Bufalo, USMC (Ret)*

"Only part of this medal belongs to me. Pieces of it belong to the boys who are still on Guadalcanal."
- *'Manila' John Basilone, upon being awarded the Medal of Honor*

"I Love it, sir!" - *A young lance corporal who was asked by a reporter about how it felt to be in Iraq and under rifle fire*

"The first time you blow someone away is not an insignificant event. That said, there are some assholes in the world that just *need* to be shot." - *Major General Jim Mattis, USMC, Iraq*

"Marine units are like giant families, and families do not dismiss tragedy. They embrace it. There's a sweet-and-sour mix of pride and despair that accompanies the memory of bravery under fire." - *Owen West*

"The Chief of Naval Operations would never be called a Sailor. The General of the Army would never be called a Soldier. The Chief of Staff of the Air Force would never be called an Airman. But the Commandant of the Marine Corps is damned proud to be called Marine!" - *Michael W. Rodriguez*

"A young sergeant (in Iraq), who had lost an eye in an explosion... asked his surgeon if he could open the other one... when he did, he sat up and looked at the young Marines from his fire team who were being treated for superficial shrapnel wounds in the next room... (then) he smiled, laid back down, and said, "I only have one good eye, Doc, but at least I can see that my Marines are OK!""

"I recall something I read about warmongers prior to going to Saudi Arabia in 1990. A warmonger is a person who is invincible in peace, and invisible in war. A warmonger is a man who is always ready to lay down your life for his country. Those whose names were inscribed on the Wall laid down their lives for me and my former country. They were not warmongers. I sincerely hope I have honored their sacrifice with my own service. The dead did not point the finger at anyone. The dead are blameless. They must be remembered and honored."
- *Q.X. Pham, who was evacuated from Saigon at the age of ten and became a U.S. Marine helicopter pilot*

"My only answer as to why the Marines get the toughest jobs is because the average Leatherneck is a much better fighter. He has far more guts, courage, and better officers... These boys out here have a pride in the Marine Corps, and will fight to the end no matter what the cost."
- *2nd Lt. Richard C. Kennard, Peleliu, World War II*

"The galleries are full of critics. They play no ball. They fight no fights. They make no mistakes because they attempt nothing. Down in the arena are *doers*. They make mistakes because they try many things. The man who makes no mistakes lacks boldness and the spirit of adventure. He is the one who never tries anything. He is the break on the wheel of progress. And yet it cannot be truly said he makes no mistakes in the very fact that he tries nothing, does nothing, except criticize those who do things." - *General David M. Shoup, U.S. Marine Corps*

"Being ready is not what matters. What matters is winning after you get there." - *Lieutenant General Victor H. "Brute" Krulak USMC, April 1965*

"Being a Marine is not of the flesh - but of the spirit. It is not that you wear the uniform - but rather how you feel about the uniform. In a very real sense it is a 'state of mind.'"- *Lieutenant General Ormand R. Simpson*

"Wars and battles are not lost by privates. They *win* them, but they don't *lose* them. They are lost by commanders, staffs, and troop leaders - and quite often before the battle starts." - *Brigadier General Sam Griffith, USMC*

"Most Americans have no idea of the meaning of pride; the kind of pride that comes not from what you do, or who you are, but because you belong to something so much greater than the individual himself - our Corps." - *Colonel John Ripley*

"Marines walk down the street with that salty, audacious swagger that tells the world we are roguishly handsome, cocky, conceited, self-centered, overbearing, mean, amphibious, S.O.B.s whose sole purpose in life is to perpetrate hellacious, romping, stomping, death and destruction upon the festering sores of America's enemies around the globe." - *Colonel "Irish" Egan*

"I was that which others did not want to be, I went where others feared to go, and did what others failed to do. I asked nothing from those that gave nothing, and reluctantly accepted the thought of eternal loneliness should I fail. I have cried, pained and hoped; but most of all I have lived times others would say are best forgotten. At least I can be proud of what I was and will ALWAYS be... A United States Marine!" - *Author Unknown*

"When I joined the Marine Corps, I figured I'd be a infantryman, go on liberty, drink beer, punch sailors, chase wild women, kill communists, and if I kept my boots clean and qualified with the rifle every year, I might grow up to be a gunnery sergeant." - *Retired MGySgt R. R. Keene, Leatherneck, April 1996*

"We Marines are truly blessed. We get to enjoy the sweet taste of freedom because we know its price." - *Marine veteran John Chipura, survivor of the 1983 Beirut bombing and a NY Fireman who wrote the above for the 225th Marine Corps birthday in 2000. He was later killed in Tower 2 of the World Trade Center while responding to the terrorist attack on 9-11*

QUOTES ABOUT LEADERSHIP

The Lore of the Corps

"They will salute the rank, but they will only *follow* the **man!**" - *Anonymous*

"Marine leaders - of every rank - know that issuing every man and woman a black beret - or polka-dotted boxer shorts for that matter - does absolutely nothing to promote morale, fighting spirit or combat effectiveness." - *Colonel James M. Lowe, USMC*

"Know your enemy, and know yourself." - *Sun Tzu*

"No matter how good it is, no plan survives first contact."

"One of the tests of leadership is the ability to recognize a problem before it becomes an *emergency*." - *Arnold H. Glasgow*

"All warfare is based upon deception." - *Sun Tzu*

"'I must do something' will solve a lot more problems than 'something must be done.'"

"The strength of the Pack is the Wolf, and the strength of the Wolf is the Pack." - *Rudyard Kipling*

"Improvise, adapt and overcome." - *Fictional Gunnery Sergeant Tom Highway*

"To see what is right, and not do it, is want of courage, or of principle." - *Confucius*

"If I had to rank the Leadership Traits, I'd have to place 'integrity' at the top." - *Major H.G. "Dunk" Duncan*

"Lead, follow, or get the hell out of the way – but do *something!*" - *Anonymous*

"Find a way, or make one." - *General of Carthage Hannibal Barca*

"That which does not kill you makes you stronger."
- *Friedrich Nietzsche*

"One ought never to turn one's back on a threatened danger and try to run away from it. If you do that, you will double the danger. But if you meet it promptly and without flinching, you will reduce the danger by half."
- *Sir Winston Churchill*

"The burdens of leadership are great. One of them is to be unpopular when necessary." - *General Tommy Franks*

"A battle is won by those who are firmly resolved to win it." - *Tolstoy*

"Few things can help an individual more than to place responsibility on him, and to let him know you trust him." - *Booker T. Washington*

"A good name, like good will, is attained by many actions, and may be lost by only one." - *Anonymous*

"Nearly all men can stand adversity, but if you want to test a man's character, give him power." - *President Abraham Lincoln*

"Example IS Leadership." - *Dr. Albert Schweitzer*

"A great leader never sets himself above his followers, except in carrying responsibilities." - *Anonymous*

"Don't tell me you 'didn't have time.' If you slept last night, you *had* time." - *Anonymous*

"It's not the load that breaks you down, it's the way you carry it." - *Lena Horne*

"An imperfect plan executed immediately and violently is far better than a perfect plan next week." - *General George S. Patton*

"Winners never quit, and quitters never win."
- *Anonymous*

"There are no secrets to success. It is the result of preparation, hard work and learning from failure."
- *General Colin Powell*

"Knowing the right thing to do is usually easy, but consistently doing the right thing in the face of adversity is something else. *That* is the true test of character."
- *Judith K. Molloy*

"Character is what we do when we think no one is looking." - *H. Jackson Brown, Jr.*

"You miss one hundred percent of the shots you never take." - *Wayne Gretzky*

"Talent alone won't make you a success. Neither will being in the right place at the right time, unless you are ready. The important question is: 'Are you ready'?"
- *Johnny Carson*

"If we should have to fight, we should be prepared to do so from the neck up, instead of from the neck down."
- *General James H. Doolittle, USAAF*

"Proper Prior Planning Prevents Piss Poor Performance!" - *The Seven "Ps"*

"Keep your fears to yourself, but share your courage with others!" - *Anonymous*

"The more you sweat in peace, the less you bleed in war!"
- *Anonymous*

"To ensure victory, the troops must have confidence in themselves as well as in their commanders." - *Niccolo Machiavelli, 1531*

"An army of sheep led by a lion are more to be feared than an army of lions led by a sheep." - *Chabrias, 370 B.C.*

"To the optimist, the glass is half full. To the pessimist, the glass is half-empty. To the Sergeant Major, the glass is twice as big as it needs to be." - *Anonymous*

"Once you are in the fight, it is *way* too late to wonder if this is 'a good idea.'" - *Anonymous*

"Nobody cares what you did yesterday, or what you are going to do tomorrow. What is important is what you are doing *now*." - *Captain Marion Sturkey, USMC*

"We are what we repeatedly do. Excellence, therefore, is not an act, but a habit." - *Aristotle*

"In war it is necessary that commanders be able to delay their emotions until they can afford them." - *General Tommy Franks*

"In the confrontation between the stream and the rock, the stream always wins, not through strength, but by perseverance." - *H. Jackson Brown*

"It is by what we ourselves have done, and not by what others have done for us, that we shall be remembered in after ages." - *Francis Wayland*

"The most dangerous man on the modern battlefield is not the one with the nastiest weapon. He's the one carrying the radio." - *Todd L. Glen*

"Perpetual optimism is a force multiplier."
- *General Colin Powell*

"The mothers and fathers of America will give you their sons and daughters... with the confidence in you that you will not needlessly waste their lives. And you dare not. That's the burden the mantle of leadership places upon you. You could be the person who gives the orders that will bring about the deaths of thousands and thousands of young men and women. It is an awesome responsibility. You cannot fail. You dare not fail..."
- *General H. Norman Schwarzkopf, in a speech to the Corps of Cadets on 15 May, 1991*

"Always use a pile driver to crack a nut. The pile driver doesn't sustain much damage, and the nut stays cracked." - *USMC axiom*

"With self-discipline, most anything is possible!"
- *Theodore Roosevelt*

"The mind is the limit. As long as the mind can envision the fact that you can do something, you can do it, as long as you really believe one hundred percent." - *Arnold Schwarzenegger*

"Light is the task where many share the toil." - *Homer*

"Discipline yourself, and others won't need to."
- *John Wooden*

"Whether you believe you can do a thing, or believe you can't - you are right!" - *Henry Ford*

"To win a war quickly takes long preparation."
- *Latin proverb*

"A pessimist sees the difficulty in every opportunity; an optimist sees the opportunity in every difficulty." - *Sir Winston Churchill*

"Ten soldiers wisely led will beat a hundred without a head." - *Euripides*

"Our doubts are traitors, and make us lose the good we oft might win by fearing to attempt." - *Shakespeare*

"The dumber people think you are, the more surprised they're going to be when you kill them." - *William Clayton*

"When we are debating an issue, loyalty means giving me your honest opinion, whether you think I'll like it or not. Disagreement, at this stage, stimulates me. But once a decision has been made, the debate ends. From that point on, loyalty means executing the decision as if it were your own." - *General Colin Powell*

"I've always considered myself to be a Marine who follows regulations, but sometimes situations arise which necessitate throwing away the book and applying a bit of common sense." - *Master Sergeant Andy Bufalo, USMC (Ret)*

"Don't condemn the judgment of another because it differs from your own. You may both be wrong!"
- *Anonymous*

"If you have one Marine without a field jacket and you are wearing one, you aren't much of a leader." – *Major H.G. "Dunk" Duncan*

"Why, it appears that we appointed all of our worst generals to command the armies, and we appointed all of our best generals to edit the newspapers. I mean, I found by reading a newspaper that these editor generals saw all of the defects plainly from the start, but didn't tell me until it was too late. I'm willing to yield my place to these best generals, and I'll do my best for the cause by editing a newspaper." - *Robert E. Lee (apparently the press was second-guessing military leaders even back then)*

"Call me crazy, but the last time I checked there was nothing *fair* about combat." – *Master Sergeant Andy Bufalo, USMC (Ret)*

"Tact is the rare talent for not *quite* telling the truth!"
- *Anonymous*

"I believe courage surpasses integrity as the most indispensable leadership quality in this age of 'don't ask, don't tell' politics. I'm not talking about the sort of physical courage normally associated with heroism, but *moral* courage." - *Master Sergeant Andy Bufalo, USMC (Ret)*

"He didn't care whether we wanted to do these things. He didn't care whether we could do them. We were going to do them. And we did." - *Columnist and Former Marine Fred Reed, talking about his Senior Drill Instructor at Parris Island*

"Failure always overtakes those who have the power to do something, but lack the will to act!" - *Anonymous*

"Getting 'Office Hours' made me a much better leader than I would have been otherwise – although I certainly *don't* recommend going that route as a means of self-improvement." - *Master Sergeant Andy Bufalo, USMC (Ret)*

"The best test of bearing is being seen in a shower room by a total stranger who calls you 'Sir'" - *Major H.G. "Dunk" Duncan*

"The term 'equal opportunity' is a hollow one unless it is accompanied by equal *responsibility* and equal *requirements*." - *Master Sergeant Andy Bufalo, USMC (Ret)*

"Justice is what you get when the decision is in your favor!" - *Anonymous*

"The Marine Corps is a martial organization charged with the defense of our way of life, not a laboratory for social experimentation." - *Master Sergeant Andy Bufalo, USMC (Ret)*

"If you don't know something, just say so!" - *Anonymous*

"Loyalty from the military is not about politics. We are *all* Americans. It is about the way members of the armed forces are treated by those in their (civilian) chain of command. That is what determines how troops perceive a leader." - *Master Sergeant Andy Bufalo, USMC (Ret)*

"Enthusiasm is contagious – and so is the lack of it!"
- *Anonymous*

"It takes ten 'atta-boys' to cancel out one 'aw-shit'."
- *Master Sergeant Andy Bufalo, USMC (Ret)*

"It is harder to conceal ignorance that it is to acquire knowledge!" - *Anonymous*

"Bearing is the ability to be ill at ease inconspicuously!"
- *Anonymous*

"Sometimes a drop of dedication is worth a bucket full of brains!" - *Anonymous*

"The very same Marines you are teaching today could well show up in the history books of tomorrow!" – *Master Sergeant Andy Bufalo, USMC (Ret)*

"Many of life's failures are men who did not realize how close they were to success when they gave up."
- *Anonymous*

"He who does not *give* loyalty cannot *command* it!"
- *Anonymous*

"There didn't seem to be a purpose to a lot of the games Drill Instructors played when I was a boot, but one day an incident occurred (in a South American jungle) which showed me there really *was* a method to their madness." - *Master Sergeant Andy Bufalo, USMC (Ret)*

"Setting an example is the most difficult thing about leading men in combat... you're the one they're looking at for leadership. You need to be one step ahead, and always have them on your mind. Somebody is watching everything you're doing: all of your decisions, your emotions and your actions." - *Lieutenant George J. Flynn*

"Always, always, remember that no one can take your integrity from you. You and *only* you can give it away!"
- *General Charles C. Krulak, Commandant of the Marine Corps*

"One of the most important lessons of command, if not *the* most important lesson, is that a commander can always delegate authority to someone else – but *never* responsibility." - *Master Sergeant Andy Bufalo, USMC*

"Something hard won is not easily relinquished."
- *Master Sergeant Andy Bufalo, USMC (Ret)*

"Given the same amount of intelligence, timidity will do a thousand times more damage than audacity." - *Karl von Clausewitz*

"The strength of an Army lies in strict discipline and undeviating obedience to its officers." - *Thucydides, 'History of The Peloponnesian War'*

"When the enemy advances, withdraw; when he stops, harass; when he tires, strike; when he retreats, pursue." - *Chairman Mao Zedong (Tse-tung)*

"Never interrupt your enemy when he is making a mistake." - *Napoleon Bonaparte*

"One of the most difficult things about being in command is enforcing rules and regulations with which you disagree." - *Master Sergeant Andy Bufalo, USMC (Ret)*

"The best leaders are the humble ones who are quick to accept blame, and even quicker to give credit where credit is due. Perhaps 'humility' should be added as the fifteenth leadership trait." - *Master Sergeant Andy Bufalo, USMC (Ret)*

"The Leadership Principles are a cornerstone of our Marine Corps' ethos, but if we don't take the time to really *understand* each of them they are nothing more than a list of fourteen words." - *Master Sergeant Andy Bufalo, USMC (Ret)*

"Wars and battles are not lost by privates. They *win* them, but they don't *lose* them. They are lost by commanders, staffs, and troop leaders - and quite often before the battle starts." – *Brigadier General Sam Griffith, USMC*

"A young sergeant (in Iraq), who had lost an eye in an explosion... asked his surgeon if he could open the other one... when he did, he sat up and looked at the young Marines from his fire team who were being treated for superficial shrapnel wounds in the next room... (then) he smiled, laid back down, and said, 'I only have one good eye, Doc, but at least I can see that my Marines are OK!'"

"It is better to have a known enemy than a forced ally."
- Napoleon Bonaparte

"The best leader is the one who has sense enough to pick good men to do what he wants done, and self-restraint enough to keep from meddling with them while they do it." *- Anonymous*

"Winners *make* it happen, and losers *let* it happen."
- Anonymous

"The difference between working to *win* and working *not to lose* is the difference between success and mediocrity."
- Anonymous

"We must remember that one man is much the same as another, and that he is best who is trained in the severest school." *- Thucydides*

"On the Plains of Hesitation lie the blackened bones of countless millions, who, at the dawn of victory lay down to rest, and in resting, died..." *- Anonymous*

QUOTES ABOUT COURAGE

The Lore of the Corps

"Courage is not the *absence* of fear, but the *conquest* of it!" - *Anonymous*

"If all the world were just, there would be no need of valor." - *Plutarch*

"The Spartans do not ask how many the enemy number, but where they are." - *Ages of Sparta, circa 415 BC*

"It matters not how a man dies, but how he lives." - *Samuel Johnson*

"Winners never quit, and quitters never win." - *Vince Lombardi*

"Thousands of Vietnam Veterans earned medals for bravery every day. A few were even awarded." - *Anonymous*

Upon being told that when the Persians loosed their arrows the sky went black, a Spartan warrior named Dienekes rejoined, "Then we shall fight in the shade."

"He insisted on giving his life so that forty of his fellow Marines might live and triumph. He had freely chosen loyalty above life." - *First Lieutenant Michael Stick, speaking of Corporal Larry Maxam, USMC, KIA RVN, 1968*

"If, as a people, we don't have the stomach to endure the inevitable difficulties we've faced in Iraq, how will we have the will to endure the war on terror over the long haul?" - *David Limbaugh*

"Courage is endurance, for one moment more..."
- *Anonymous*

"Courage is not having the strength to go on; it is going on, when you don't have the strength." - *Theodore Roosevelt*

"All who volunteered for the Army or Marine Corps since September 11, 2001 knew they were signing up for more than college or job training or tickets out of dead-end towns: They knew they would likely be called to lay their lives on the line." - *Lynn Vincent*

"You've done your job, Mom. Now it is *my* turn to protect *you*." - *Sergeant Byron Norwood USMC, Iraq*

"Et si fellitur de genu pugnat" (And if he falls, he fights on his knees) - *Motto of the Roman Legions*

"It is not the critic who counts, not the man who points out how the strong man stumbled, or where the doer of deeds could have done better. The credit belongs to the man who is actually in the arena; whose face is marred by the dust and sweat and blood; who strives valiantly; who errs and comes short again and again; who knows the great enthusiasms, the great devotions and spends himself in a worthy cause; who at the best, knows in the end the triumph of high achievement, and who, at worst, if he fails, at least fails while daring greatly; so that his place shall never be with those cold and timid souls who know neither victory or defeat." - *Theodore Roosevelt*

"We few, we happy few, we band of brothers; For he today that sheds his blood with me shall be my brother."
- *William Shakespeare*

"One ought never to turn one's back on a threatened danger and try to run away from it. If you do that, you will double the danger. But if you meet it promptly and without flinching, you will reduce the danger by half."
- *Sir Winston Churchill*

"Being defeated is often a temporary condition. *Giving up is what makes it permanent.*" - *Marilyn vos Savant*

"It's not the size of the man in the fight, it's the size of the fight in the man!" - *Anonymous*

"You can never surrender too early, or too often." - *Rule of French warfare*

"When you men get home and face an anti-war protester, look him in the eyes and shake his hand. Then, wink at his girlfriend, because she knows she's dating a pussy."
- *Attributed to General Tommy Franks*

"All that is necessary for evil to succeed is that good men do nothing." - *Edmund Burke*

"Knowing the right thing to do is usually easy, but consistently doing the right thing in the face of adversity is something else. That is the true test of character."
- *Judith K. Molloy*

"A hero is no braver than the ordinary man, but he is braver five minutes longer." – *Ralph Waldo Emerson*

"Far better it is to dare mighty things, to win glorious triumphs even though checkered by failure, than to rank with those poor spirits who neither enjoy nor suffer much because they live in the gray twilight that knows neither victory nor defeat." - *President Theodore Roosevelt*

"We Marines have always prided ourselves on being squared away, positive role models. We have the Silent Drill Platoon. We spit shine our boots. We field day our barracks until you can eat off the deck, and stand wall locker inspections where one 'Irish pennant' is cause for failure. But the thing we admire above all else is personal heroism." - *Master Sergeant Andy Bufalo, USMC (Ret)*

"He who lives only for himself does not have very much to live for." - *Anonymous*

"If you can find humor in anything, you can survive it."
- *Comedian and former FMF Corpsman Bill Cosby*

"The only thing we have to fear is fear itself – the nameless, unreasoning, unjustified terror which paralyzes needed efforts to convert retreat into advance."
- *President Franklin D. Roosevelt*

"I think it is better to do right, even if we suffer in so doing, than to incur the reproach of our consciences and posterity." - *Robert E. Lee*

"The ultimate measure of a man is not where he stands in moments of comfort, but where he stands at times of challenge and controversy." - *Dr. Martin Luther King, Jr.*

"Cowards die many times before their deaths; The valiant never taste death but once." - *William Shakespeare*

"Heroes are people who rise to the occasion and quietly slip away." - *Tom Brokaw*

"It is time for us to stand and cheer for the doer, the achiever, the one who recognizes the challenge and does something about it." - *Vince Lombardi*

"The world has no room for cowards. We must all be ready somehow to toil, to suffer, to die. And yours is not the less noble because no drum beats before you when you go out into your daily battlefields, and no crowds shout about your coming when you return from your daily victory or defeat." - *Robert Lewis Stevenson*

"Marine units are like giant families, and families do not dismiss tragedy. They embrace it. There's a sweet-and-sour mix of pride and despair that accompanies the memory of bravery under fire." - *Owen West*

"Keep your fears to yourself, but share your courage with others!" - *Anonymous*

"Without a sign, his sword the brave man draws, and asks no omen, but his country's cause." – *Homer*

"True heroism isn't a matter of chance. It's a matter of choice!" – *Peter Lemmon*

"Almighty Father... if I am inclined to doubt, steady my faith. If I am tempted, make me strong to resist. If I should miss the mark, give me courage to try again..."
- *From "The Marines' Prayer"*

"Of all that is written, I love only what a person has written with his own blood." - *Friedrich Nietzsche*

"A man who won't die for something is not fit to live."
- *Dr. Martin Luther King, Jr.*

"Where do they get young men like this?" - *Martin Savidge of CNN, while embedded with the 1st Marine Division in Iraq*

"True heroism is remarkably sober, very undramatic. It is not the urge to surpass all others at whatever cost, but the urge to serve others at whatever cost." - *Arthur Ashe*

"When I was a little boy my third grade teacher told me that my dad was a hero. When I went home and told my dad that, he looked at me and said, 'I want you always to remember that the heroes of Iwo Jima are the guys who did not come back. Did *not* come back.'" - *James Bradley, author of 'Flags of Our Fathers' and son of Iwo Jima flag-raiser John Bradley*

"I believe courage surpasses integrity as the most indispensable leadership quality in this age of "don't ask, don't tell" politics. I'm not talking about the sort of physical courage normally associated with heroism, but *moral* courage." - *Master Sergeant Andy Bufalo, USMC*

"Men under fire rarely speak of glory. Instead, they speak of, 'who can be counted upon, and who cannot.' Above all, they speak about and remember the small individual acts of selflessness." - *General Charles C. Krulak, USMC Commandant*

"America is the land of the free, *because* of the brave!"
- *Tattoo on the arm of a U.S. Marine in Iraq*

"Visions haunt me every day, not of the nightmares of war but of the steady consistency with which my Marines faced their responsibilities, and of how uncomplaining most of them were in the face of constant danger... these Marines were the finest people I have ever been around... It would be redundant to say that I would trust my life to these men... because I already have, in more ways than I can ever recount. I am alive today because of their quiet, unaffected heroism." - *James Webb*

"The Marines did a tremendous job. While most people were running *out* of the building, they were running *in*, despite the obvious danger." - *A senior State Department official, in the aftermath of our embassy in Nairobi being bombed by terrorists*

"Somewhere, somehow, he had taken the words honor, courage and commitment into his very soul and laid his life on the line daily for me and us... I realized I had rubbed shoulders with greatness in the flesh and in the twinkling of an eye my life was forever changed. His name is Michael Mendez, a corporal in the USMC. We are a great nation. We know because the makings of it walked into my office that day." - *Ann Baker of Huntington Beach, California in a letter to the Orange County Register on June 30, 2002*

"When men find they must inevitably perish, they willingly resolve to die with their comrades and with their arms in their hands." - *Flavius Vegetius Renatus*

QUOTES BY CELEBRITIES
Who were (*are*) Marines

Plus one guy who didn't *quite* make it...

The Lore of the Corps

"The thing I'm most proud of is that I was a Marine Corps fighter pilot." - *Baseball great Ted Williams*

"My pride in the Marine Corps has never diminished."
- *Ed McMahon*

"I was a PFC in the Marine Corps, so when I started playing officers (in the movies) I had a good opinion as to how they should be portrayed – from the bias of an enlisted man's viewpoint." - *Lee Marvin*

"I liked being in the Marines. They gave me discipline I could live with... sure I was pretty wild – but I had a lot of rough edges knocked off." - *Steve McQueen*

"Whatever else we are or may become for the rest of our lives, if you have once been a Marine, you are always a Marine." - *James Brady*

"I'd give a million dollars to be a Marine." - *Former heavyweight boxing champion Riddick Bowe (he lasted eleven days at Parris Island before he quit)*

"My Marine Corps experience means a great deal to me in many ways. The camaraderie, discipline and tenacity I learned helped me face some awful situations in my life."
- *Actor and former Marine Gerald O'Loughlin (TV's 'The Rookies')*

"(My Marine Corps service) was the first time I had a real sense of pride about myself, a sense of belonging to a group that's special. To this day, I'm proud of being a Marine." - *Actor and former Marine Harvey Keitel*

"My Marine Corps experience has served me well. Everyone has heard about the pride of the Marines. Through training, both physical and psychological, we were given a very positive feeling about our capabilities. A very high esteem, something more parents should give their children." - *Former Marine Bob Keeshan (Captain Kangaroo)*

"I have drawn inspiration from the Marine Corps, the Jewish struggle in Palestine and Israel, and the Irish." - *Bestselling Author Leon Uris*

"I've always been proud of being a Marine. I won't hesitate to defend the Corps." - *Jonathan Winters*

"My guiding thought throughout (writing 'Battle Cry') was that the real Marine story had not been told. We were a different breed of men who looked at war in a different way." - *Bestselling Author and Former Marine Leon Uris*

"I firmly believe that becoming a Marine was the defining experience of my life. Any success I have achieved, I feel I owe in no small measure to the values and principles I learned in the Marine Corps." - *Actor and former Marine Joe Lisi (Lt. Swersky on TV's 'Third Watch')*

QUOTES BY POLITICIANS

The Lore of the Corps

"I served twenty-three years in the United States Marine Corps. I served through two wars. I flew 149 combat missions. My plane was hit by antiaircraft fire on twelve different occasions... I *have* held a job, Howard! What about you?" - *Senator John Glenn's reply to Howard Metzenbaum, a wealthy, self-made millionaire who had accused Glenn, as a 'lifetime government employee,' of never having held a job.*

"Congressmen who willfully take actions during wartime that damage morale and undermine the military are saboteurs and should be arrested, exiled, or hanged." - *President Abraham Lincoln*

"The U.S. Marine Corps has a propaganda machine to rival Stalin's." - *President Harry S. Truman*

"You will never know how much it has cost my generation to preserve your freedom. I hope you will use it wisely." - *John Adams*

"Those of us who have had the privilege of serving in the Marine Corps value our experience as among the most precious of our lives. The fellowship of shared hardships and dangers in a worthy cause creates a close bond of comradeship. It is the basic reason for the cohesiveness of Marines and for the pride we have in our Corps and our loyalty to each other." - *Senator and Former Marine Paul H. Douglas*

"Courage is not having the strength to go on; it is going on, when you don't have the strength." - *Theodore Roosevelt*

"My experience in the United States Marine Corps steered me onto the path of success. The Marine Corps instilled in me honor, courage and commitment - core values that have sustained me through thick and thin."
- *Senator Zell Miller*

"I pray that our Heavenly Father may assuage the anguish of your bereavement, and leave you only the cherished memory of the loved and lost, and the solemn pride that must be yours to have laid so costly a sacrifice upon the alter of freedom." - *From President Abraham Lincoln's letter to a mother who had lost five sons in the Civil War*

"The eyes of the nation and the eyes of the entire world, the eyes of history itself, are on that brave little band of defenders who hold the pass at Khe Sahn." - *President Lyndon Johnson*

"Some people spend an entire lifetime wondering if they made a difference in the world. But, the Marines don't have that problem." - *Ronald Reagan, President of the United States; 1985*

"All who now wear, or have ever worn, the eagle, globe and anchor share a common bond." - *Senator and former Marine Charles Robb*

"Today, the world looks to America for leadership. And America looks to its Corps of Marines." - *President Ronald Reagan*

"Here's my strategy on the Cold War: We win, they lose." - *President Ronald Reagan*

"There is no better group of fighting men anywhere in the world than in the Marine Corps." - *Senator Irving M. Ives*

"It is friendship, and something beyond friendship, that binds the Marine Corps together." - *Secretary of State Donald Regan*

"Those who are wringing their hands and shouting so loudly for 'heads to roll' over [the Iraq prison abuse] seem to have conveniently overlooked the fact that someone's head *has* rolled - that of another innocent American brutally murdered by terrorists. Why is it that there's more indignation over a photo of a prisoner with underwear on his head, than over the video of a young American with no head at all?" - *Senator Zell Miller*

"Of the four wars in my lifetime, none came about because the U.S. was too *strong*."-- *President Ronald Reagan*

"Do not yield. Do not flinch. Stand up. Stand up with our President and fight. We're Americans. We're Americans, and we'll never surrender. They will." - *Senator John McCain*

"I say to our enemies, God may show you mercy. We will not." - *Senator John McCain, 12 September 2001*

QUOTES ABOUT THE WAR ON TERRORISM

The Lore of the Corps

"I say to our enemies, God may show you mercy. We will not." - *Senator John McCain, 12 September 2001*

"We sometimes forget, but freedom isn't free." - *Johnny Spann, father of CIA officer & Former Marine Mike Spann, who was the first U.S. casualty in the war on terrorism*

"We signed up knowing the risk. Those innocent people in New York didn't go to work thinking there was any kind of risk." - *Private Mike Armendariz-Clark, USMC in September, 2001*

"Have you forgotten how it felt that day? To see your homeland under fire, and her people blown away. Have you forgotten when those towers fell? We had neighbors still inside going thru a living hell. And you say we shouldn't worry 'bout bin Laden. Have you forgotten?"
- *Darryl Worley in his song "Have You Forgotten?"*

"There is no terrorist threat." - *"Film maker" Michael Moore (How then does he explain the smoking holes in the ground where the twin towers and our embassies in Nairobi, Dar es Salaam and Beirut once stood?)*

"The death of one man is a tragedy. The death of millions is a statistic." - *Joseph Stalin*

"We are at last standing up against a modern day Hitler and using our fist. If we had done something positive the first time the Trade Center was bombed, we would have six thousand more citizens today." - *Medal of Honor recipient Colonel Wesley Fox, USMC*

"Sometimes it takes good people killing bad people to keep bad people from killing good people." - *Phil Messina* "I am sorry that the last seven times we Americans took up arms and sacrificed the blood of our youth, it was in the defense of Muslims." - *Attributed to Lieutenant General Chuck Pittman USMC (Ret)*

"This is a time for all Americans to reflect on what it means to be an American. We have gone across the seas in years past to fight in the defense of the freedoms we hold so dear, but this time the battlefield is closer to home - too close." - *Medal of Honor recipient Colonel Harvey C. "Barney" Barnum USMC*

"We did not seek this war on terror, but this is the world as we find it. We must keep our focus. We must do our duty. History is moving, and it will tend toward hope, or tend toward tragedy." - *President George W. Bush*

"For the last ten years, we Americans have been hit numerous times by terrorists with the resulting loss of many lives. We knew who were behind the acts and we negotiated, we talked. Our good intentions were for nothing; we are seen as ineffective, as paper tigers, so we are slapped harder. Some people who share our world understand and respect only the fist, not words." - *Colonel Wesley Fox USMC (Ret)*

"All who volunteered for the Army or Marine Corps since September 11, 2001, knew they were signing up for more than college, or job training, or tickets out of dead-end towns: They knew they would likely be called to lay their lives on the line." - *Lynn Vincent*

"Today, all Americans are united in anguish and anger. But we must also be united in purpose and in will. While the immediate task of vanquishing freedom's enemies will fall to our military men and women, all of us - particularly those like you who understand the price of freedom - will be called upon to strengthen our national resolve." - *Secretary of Defense Donald Rumsfeld*

"We're not running out of [fixed] targets. Afghanistan is." - *Secretary of Defense Donald Rumsfeld, October 9, 2001*

"If, as a people, we don't have the stomach to endure the inevitable difficulties we've faced in Iraq, how will we have the will to endure the war on terror over the long haul?" - *David Limbaugh*

"The warrior has come center stage once again, and it is time for the tender-hearted to take a seat and be quiet. The warrior will ensure that they, the talkers, retain all of their rights, to include letting the warrior do the tough, ugly work." - *Colonel Wesley Fox on fighting the 'War on Terrorism'*

"Do not yield. Do not flinch. Stand up. Stand up with our President and fight. We're Americans. We're Americans, and we'll never surrender. They will." - *Senator John McCain*

"It must be puzzling to our enemies as to how the bravery of the warriors they face in combat can be offset by the cowardly and self-serving behavior those far from harm's way publicly display at every opportunity." - *Captain Dave St. John, USMCR*

"Less than three years after America began to face down the greatest threat yet to our national survival, not only has half the country given up the fight, but they have closed their eyes to the danger." - *Tony Blankley*

"It's God's job to forgive Bin Laden. It's the Marine Corps' job to arrange the meeting." - *Anonymous*

"Conservatives saw the savagery of 9/11 in the attacks and prepared for war; liberals saw the savagery of the 9/11 attacks and wanted to prepare indictments, and offer therapy and understanding for our attackers... Al Jazeera now broadcasts the words of Senator Durbin to the Mideast, certainly putting our troops in greater danger." - *Karl Rove*

"One of the most important parts of Marine Corps training teaches the Law of War, which dictates how we are supposed to conduct ourselves on the battlefield. They say all is fair in love and war, but that isn't exactly true. Combat, while brutal, does have guidelines of gentlemanly conduct, and any nation that fails to observe them is considered a terrorist state." - *Master Sergeant Andy Bufalo, USMC (Ret)*

"It is a sad commentary on our society when more tears were shed in this country over the last episode of 'Friends' than over the videotaped beheading of an innocent American by murderous terrorists. Perhaps more people would have cared if his murder had been part of a reality TV series." - *Master Sergeant Andy Bufalo, USMC (Ret)*

"They have no moral inhibition on the slaughter of the innocent. If they could have murdered not seven thousand, but *seventy* thousand, does anyone doubt they would have done so, and rejoiced in it?" - *British Prime Minister Tony Blair*

"If hooking up an terrorist's scrotum to a car's battery cables will save one American life, then I have just two things to say: 'Red is positive, and black is negative.'" - *T. "Bubba" Bechtol, part time City Councilman from Pensacola, Florida*

"Terrorists look at America and see a soft target, and to a large extent they are right. Our country is filled with a lot of spoiled people who drive BMWs, sip decaf lattes and watch ridiculous reality TV shows. They are for the most part decent, hard working citizens, but they are soft... (but) we also have a warrior culture in this country, and they are called Marines. It is a brotherhood forged in the fire of many wars, and the bond between us is stronger than blood." - *Master Sergeant Andy Bufalo, USMC (Ret)*

"If you think the Marines were tough on you when they were cleaning out Fallujah a few weeks ago you haven't seen anything yet. If you want to know what it feels like to have the Wrath of God called down upon you then go ahead and do it (behead a captured Marine)... We are the United States Marines, and we will be coming for you." - *Master Sergeant Andy Bufalo, USMC (Ret) in an open letter to terrorists*

"U.S. Marines: Travel agents to Allah." - *Bumper Sticker*

"On the Plains of Hesitation lie the blackened bones of countless millions, who, at the dawn of victory lay down to rest, and in resting, died..." - *Anonymous*

QUOTES ABOUT FREEDOM

The Lore of the Corps

"Shall I tell you what the real evil is? To cringe to the things that are called evils, to surrender to them our freedom, in defiance of which we ought to face any suffering." - *Lucius Annaeus Seneca*

"Freedom is the sure possession of only those who have the courage to defend it!" - *Anonymous*

"We sometimes forget, but freedom isn't free." - *Johnny Spann, father of CIA officer & Former Marine Mike Spann, who was the first U.S. casualty in the war on terrorism*

"None can love freedom heartily, but good men; the rest love not freedom, but license." - *John Milton*

"The words 'United We Stand' do not apply only to Americans - they apply to *all* who love freedom."
- *Master Sergeant Andy Bufalo, USMC (Ret)*

"To see what is right, and not do it, is want of courage, or of principle." - *Confucius*

"You will never know how much it has cost my generation to preserve your freedom. I hope you will use it wisely." - *John Adams*

"The Tree of Liberty must be watered from time to time with the blood of Patriots and tyrants." - *Thomas Jefferson*

"It is a common observation here that our cause is the cause of all mankind, and that we are fighting for their liberty in defending our own." - *Benjamin Franklin*

"Eternal vigilance is the price of liberty." - *Wendell Phillips*

"Life, Liberty, and the Pursuit of all who threaten them."
- *A new motto for our times*

"America must win this war. Therefore, I will work, I will save, I will sacrifice, I will endure, I will fight cheerfully and do my utmost, as if the issue of the whole struggle depended on me alone." - *Martin Treptow, 1917*

"There is a true glory and a true honor; the glory of duty done, the honor of the integrity of principle." - *Robert E. Lee*

"These are the times that try men's souls. The summer soldier and the sunshine patriot will, in this crisis, shrink from the service of his country; but he that stands by it now, deserves the love and thanks of man and woman."
- *Thomas Paine*

"We, too, born to freedom, and believing in freedom, are willing to fight to maintain freedom. We, and all others who believe as deeply as we do, would rather die on our feet than live on our knees." - *Franklin Delano Roosevelt*

"A man who will not protect his freedom does not deserve to be free." - *General Douglas MacArthur*

"We must indeed all hang together, or most assuredly we shall all hang separately." - *Benjamin Franklin*

"Those who expect to reap the blessings of liberty must, like men, undergo the fatigue of supporting it." - *Thomas Paine*

"A man's country is not just an area of land. It's a principle, and patriotism is loyalty to that principle."
- *Anonymous*

"Today, we need a nation of Minutemen, citizens who are not only prepared to take arms, but citizens who regard the preservation of freedom as the basic purpose of their daily life and who are willing to consciously work and sacrifice for that freedom." - *John F. Kennedy*

"All that is necessary for evil to succeed is that good men do nothing." – *Edmund Burke*

"We in this country, in this generation, are by destiny rather than choice the watchmen on the walls of world freedom. We ask therefore, that we may be worthy of our power and responsibility, that we may exercise our strength with wisdom and restraint, and that we may achieve in our time and for all time the ancient vision of peace on earth, goodwill toward men." - *John F. Kennedy (from a speech that was never delivered, due to Kennedy's death)*

"I do not approve of a word you say, but will defend to the death your right to say it." - *Voltaire*

"May all of us become an efficient, patriotic, and nobly proud people - too proud either to inflict wrong, or to endure it." - *Theodore Roosevelt*

"America is great because America is good. When America ceases to be good, America will cease to be great." - *Alexis de Tocqueville*

"I only regret that I have but one life to lose for my country." - *Nathan Hale, before being hanged by the British, 1776*

"Let every nation know, whether it wishes us well or ill, that we shall pay any price, bear any burden, meet any hardship, support any friend, oppose any foe, to assure the survival and success of liberty." - *President John F. Kennedy*

"Be convinced that to be happy means to be free, and that to be free means to be brave. Therefore do not take lightly the perils of war."- *Thucydides*

"No arsenal, or no weapon in the arsenals of the world, is so formidable as the will and moral courage of free men and women." - *Ronald Reagan*

"The man who has not raised himself to be a soldier, and the woman who has not raised her boy to be a soldier, neither of them has the right or is entitled to the citizenship of the Republic." - *Theodore Roosevelt*

"For those who fight for it, freedom has a flavor the protected never know." - *Written on a C-ration box at Khe Sanh, South Vietnam, 1968*

QUOTES ABOUT WAR & PEACE

The Lore of the Corps

"People sleep peaceably in their beds at night only because rough men stand ready to do violence on their behalf." - *George Orwell*

"Let us recollect that peace or war will not always be left to our option; that however moderate or unambitious we may be, we cannot count upon the moderation, or hope to extinguish the ambition of others." - *Alexander Hamilton*

"Let him who desires peace prepare for war."- *Vegetius, Roman military strategist*

"Except for ending slavery, Fascism, Nazism, and Communism, war has never solved *anything*."
- *Anonymous*

"The legitimate object of war is a more perfect peace."
- *William Tecumseh Sherman*

"War is the remedy our enemies have chosen. And I say, let us give them all they want." - *William Tecumseh Sherman, 1864*

"War is an ugly thing, but not the ugliest of things. The decayed and degraded state of moral and patriotic feeling which thinks that nothing is worth war is much worse. The person who has nothing for which he is willing to fight, nothing which is more important than his own personal safety, is a miserable creature and has no chance of being free unless made and kept so by the exertions of better men than himself." - *John Stewart Mill*

"Here's my strategy on the Cold War: We win, they lose." - *President Ronald Reagan*

"Of the four wars in my lifetime, none came about because the U.S. was too *strong*." - *President Ronald Reagan*

"War educates the senses, calls into action the will, perfects the physical constitution, brings men into such swift and close collision in critical moments that man measures man." - *Emerson*

"When the soldier comes home, what he remembers is a fraction of what he forgets; and what he forgets is what he chooses not to remember" - *Nelson DeMille's 'Word Of Honor'*

"A man will fight long and hard for a bit of colored ribbon." - *Napoleon Bonaparte*

"The warrior has come center stage once again, and it is time for the tender-hearted to take a seat and be quiet. The warrior will ensure that they, the talkers, retain all of their rights, to include letting the warrior do the tough, ugly work." - *Colonel Wesley Fox USMC (Ret), Medal of Honor recipient*

"Every molly-coddle, professional pacifist, and man who is 'too proud to fight' when the nation's quarrel is just, should be exiled to those out of the way parts... where the spirit of manliness has not yet penetrated." - *Theodore Roosevelt*

"The soldier above all others prays for peace, for it is the soldier who must suffer and bear the deepest wounds and scars of war." - *General Douglas MacArthur*

"For it's Tommy this, and Tommy that, and 'Chuck him out, the brute!' But it's 'Saviour of his country' when the guns begin to shoot; And it's Tommy this, and Tommy that, and anything you please; And Tommy ain't a bloomin' fool - you bet that Tommy sees!" - *Rudyard Kipling*

"There are those who believe that men in uniform are somehow associated with starting wars. That's like saying policemen cause crime... Keeping the peace is the most important problem we face. And I believe that because young men... are willing to put on the uniform and endure the rigors of military life, peace is more secure." - *President Ronald Reagan*

"Don't be a fool and die for your country. Make the other poor, dumb sonofabitch die for *his*." - *General George S. Patton*

"If peace cannot be maintained with honor, it is no longer peace." - *Lord John Russell*

"Never in the course of human conflict was so much owed by so many to so few." - *Sir Winston Churchill*

"Although war is evil, it is occasionally the lesser of two evils." - *McGeorge Bundy*

"In war, there are no unwounded soldiers."- *Jose Narosky*

"If all the world were just, there would be no need of valor." - *Plutarch*

"We will never forgive you for making us kill your sons."
- *Israeli Prime-Minister Golda Meir, addressing the Arab nations*

"Once we have a war there is only one thing to do. It must be won. For defeat brings worse things than any that can ever happen in war." - *Ernest Hemingway*

"War can only be abolished by war, and in order to get rid of the gun it is necessary to take up the gun."
- *Chairman Mao Zedong (Tse-tung)*

"He that makes war without many mistakes has not made war very long." - *Napoleon Bonaparte*

"The greatest happiness is to vanquish your enemies, to chase them before you, to rob them of their wealth, to see those dear to them bathed in tears, to clasp to your bosom their wives and daughters. - *Genghis Khan, 13th century*

"I recall something I read about warmongers prior to going to Saudi Arabia in 1990. A warmonger is a person who is invincible in peace, and invisible in war. A warmonger is a man who is always ready to lay down your life for his country. Those whose names were inscribed on the Wall laid down their lives for me and my former country. They were not warmongers. I sincerely hope I have honored their sacrifice with my own service. The dead did not point the finger at anyone. The dead are blameless. They must be remembered and honored."
- *Q.X. Pham, who was evacuated from Saigon at the age of ten and became a U.S. Marine helicopter pilot*

"There is only one decisive victory: the last."
- *Karl von Clausewitz*

"If you think violence never solved anything, go ask the Carthaginians." - *Robert Heinlein*

The Lore of the Corps

REMEMBERING
THE FALLEN

The Lore of the Corps

"Go Stranger and tell the Spartans: faithful, here we fell." - *Inscription at Thermopayle*

"We have gone forth from our shores repeatedly over the last hundred years and we've done this as recently as the last year in Afghanistan and put wonderful young men and women at risk, many of whom have lost their lives, and we have asked for nothing except enough ground to bury them in." - *Colin Powell*

"If you are able, save for them a place inside of you and save one backward glance when you are leaving for the places they can no longer go. Be not ashamed to say you loved them, though you may or may not have always. Take what they have taught you with their dying and keep it with your own. And in that time when men decide and feel safe to call the war insane, take one moment to embrace those gentle heroes you left behind." - *Major Michael O'Donnell USMC, KIA March 24, 1970 in Dak To, Vietnam*

"I pray that our Heavenly Father may assuage the anguish of your bereavement, and leave you only the cherished memory of the loved and lost, and the solemn pride that must be yours to have laid so costly a sacrifice upon the alter of freedom." - *Excerpt from President Abraham Lincoln's letter to a mother who had lost five sons in the Civil War*

"They summed up and perfected, by one supreme act, the highest virtues of men and citizens. For love of country they accepted death, and thus resolved all doubts, and made immortal their patriotism and virtue." - *General James A. Garfield*

"Poor is the nation that has no heroes, but *beggared* is the nation that has, and forgets them." - *Anonymous*

"For those beneath the wooden crosses, there is nothing we can do, except perhaps to pause and murmur, 'Thanks pal, thanks.'" - *Ernie Pyle*

"It is foolish and wrong to mourn the men who died. Rather we should thank God that such men *lived*." - *General George S. Patton*

"Here rests in honored glory an American soldier known but to God." - *Inscription on the Tomb of the Unknown Soldier*

"They Came in Peace" - *A stretcher bearing a wreath and the sign "24 MAU: They Came in Peace" was put up soon after recovery operation on the site of the bombed out BLT headquarters building began in Beirut*

"They shall not grow old, as we who are left grow old. Age shall not weary them, nor the years condemn. At the going down of the sun, and in the morning, we will remember them." - *Lawrence Binyon (Australian Ode to War Dead)*

"You are not forgotten." - *Words on the POW/MIA Flag*

QUOTES FROM BOOKS, MOVIES & SONG

"I have neither the time nor the inclination to explain myself to a man who rises and sleeps under the blanket of the very freedom which I provide, and then questions the manner in which I provide it. I would rather you just said 'thank you' and went on your way." - *Fictional Colonel Nathan Jessup (portrayed by Jack Nicholson) in 'A Few Good Men'*

"I am here to turn you slimy civilian cesspool parasites into Marine Corps space aviators, invoking bowel wrenching fear into the dark hearts of your enemies." - *My 'co-star,' mythical Sergeant Major Boguss (played by R. Lee Ermy) in the film 'Space'*

"You will not like me, but the more you hate me, the more you will learn." - *Drill Instructor Gunnery Sergeant Hartman (R. Lee Ermy) in 'Full Metal Jacket'*

"Improvise, adapt and overcome." - *Fictional Gunnery Sergeant Tom Highway in 'Heartbreak Ridge'*

"To the Corps elite, to that special breed of sky devil known and feared throughout the world, the Marine dogfighter, the bravest men who have ever lived. There is not a force that can defeat us in battle, deny us victory, or interrupt our destiny. Marines!" - *Toast made by Lieutenant Colonel W.P. "Bull" Meecham, aka "The Great Santini"*

"A committee of Congressmen, who asshole to asshole couldn't make a beer fart in a whirlwind..." - *Mythical Gunnery Sergeant Tom Highway (as portrayed by Clint Eastwood) in the film 'Heartbreak Ridge'*

"Walk softly and carry an armored tank battalion."
- *Fictional Colonel Nathan Jessup from the film 'A Few Good Men'*

"Jumping out of a perfectly good aircraft is not a natural act. Just do it right and enjoy the view." - *Mythical Gunnery Sergeant Tom Highway (played by Clint Eastwood) in the film 'Heartbreak Ridge'*

"Marines die, that's what we're here for. But the Marine Corps lives forever. And that means YOU live forever."
- *Mythical GySgt Hartman (portrayed by R. Lee Ermey) in the film 'Full Metal Jacket'*

"You call that a salute, mister? I call it an abortion. I call that a disgrace. I call that an insult to a Marine Corps officer. I call that a court-martial offense. Now straighten up that arm, get that elbow up, and don't bend your neck to the right... make it snap... old Marines should have arthritic elbows from snapping salutes... if I ever see you give me one of those spaghetti salutes again I'm going to have your arm amputated up to the shoulder!" – *'The Great Santini,' to a sentry who had just rendered a sub-par salute - from the book of the same name*

"And yes, I do have questions, I get to ask them because I'm free. That's why I've got a sticker for the U.S. Marines, on the bumper of my S.U.V." - *From the song 'Bumper of My S.U.V.' by Chely Wright*

"If you do something I don't like I'm gonna jump, and when I land it'll hurt. I'll ride you until you can't stand up. When you do, you'll be Marines." – *John Wayne as 'Sergeant Stryker' in 'The Sands of Iwo Jima'*

"His name was Joe Enders, from south Philadelphia. He was a fierce warrior, a good Marine. If you ever tell a story about him George... say he was my friend." - *Navajo 'Ben Yahzee' in the film 'Wind Talkers'*

"Have you forgotten how it felt that day? To see your homeland under fire, and her people blown away. Have you forgotten when those towers fell? We had neighbors still inside going thru a living hell. And you say we shouldn't worry 'bout bin Laden... Have you forgotten?" - *Darryl Worley in his song 'Have You Forgotten?'*

"All gave some, and some gave all. Some stood through for the red, white and blue, and some had to fall. If you ever think of me, think of all your liberties and recall, some gave all." - *Billy Ray Cyrus, from the song 'Some Gave All'*

"They battled up Iwo Jima hill, two-hundred and fifty men, but only twenty-seven lived, to walk back down again..." - *From 'The Ballad of Ira Hayes' (Written by Peter LaFarge and recorded by Johnny Cash)*

"Hold your ground! Hold your ground!... I see in your eyes the same fear that would take the heart of me! A day may come, when the courage of men fails, when we forsake our friends and break all bonds of fellowship, but it is not this day! This day we fight!" - *Aragorn, 'Lord of the Rings'*

"Only a Marine would dare look like that around here. He must be a bad-ass dude." - *From 'Fields of Fire' by James Webb*

"The only time the Navy and the Marine Corps are on the same side is in time of war, and during the Army-Navy game!" - *The Great Santini*

"Hell Private Joker, I like you. You can come over to my house and f**k my sister!" - *Drill Instructor Gunnery Sergeant Hartman in 'Full Metal Jacket'*

"Pay attention. Stay alert. Stay alive. It's as simple as that." – *R. Lee Ermey as the Sergeant Major in 'Siege of Firebase Gloria'*

"You don't want the truth because deep down in places you don't talk about at parties you want me on that wall, you *need* me on that wall. We use words like honor, code, loyalty. We use them as the backbone of a life trying to defend something. You use them as a punchline."
- *Fictional Colonel Nathan Jessup from the film 'A Few Good Men'*

"You joined the Marines because you wanted to fight. Well, you're going to get your chance." – *John Wayne as Sergeant Stryker in 'The Sands of Iwo Jima'*

"Only two things come out of Oklahoma. Steers, and queers. Which one are you, boy? I don't see no horns, so you must be a queer." – *Lou Gossett Jr. as Gunnery Sergeant Foley in 'An Officer and a Gentleman'*

"Good shooting, Marines!" – *Arnold Schwarzenegger to Marine Harrier pilots who had just knocked out a bridge being crossed by terrorists in 'True Lies'*

"I don't believe what I'm seeing! Where have you been all your lives, at an orgy? Listening to Mick Jagger music and bad mouthing your country, I'll bet!" - *Lou Gossett Jr. as Gunnery Sergeant Foley in 'An Officer and a Gentleman'*

"You murdered that poor little old sand flea after I told you to let it eat all it wanted, didn't you?" - *Jack Webb as T/Sgt Jim Moore in 'The DI'*

"Be advised that I'm mean, nasty and tired. I eat concertina wire and piss napalm, and can put a round through a flea's ass at two-hundred meters." - *Gunnery Sergeant Tom Highway (played by Clint Eastwood) in the film 'Heartbreak Ridge'*

"You burr-headed idiots do not appreciate my cheerful good morning!" - *Jack Webb as T/Sgt Jim Moore in 'The DI'*

"You people ain't even a mob. A mob's got a leader. You clowns are a *herd*. I'm going to get me a sheepdog!" - *Jack Webb as T/Sgt Jim Moore in 'The DI'*

"We don't try in the Marine Corps. We either do, or we don't. We don't straddle any fences." - *Jack Webb as T/Sgt Jim Moore in 'The DI'*

"Captain Jerome, United States Marine Corps... and you are my prisoner, sir!" - *From the movie 'Wind and the Lion'*

"Maybe we have a responsibility as officers to train Santiago. Maybe we have a responsibility to this country to see that the men and women charged with its security are trained professionals. Yes, I'm certain that I read that somewhere once." - *Colonel Nathan Jessup (portrayed by Jack Nicholson) in 'A Few Good Men'*

"Private Joker is silly and he is ignorant but he's got guts, and guts is enough!" - *Drill Instructor Gunnery Sergeant Hartman (R. Lee Ermey) in 'Full Metal Jacket'*

"His brother would go on about the Corps as if it were a combination of the Knights of the Round Table and the Jesse James gang, rough and ribald and yet steeped in the purest form of camaraderie." - *From 'A Sense of Honor' by James Webb*

"Your rifle is only a tool. It is a hard heart that kills!" - *Drill Instructor Gunnery Sergeant Hartman (R. Lee Ermey) in 'Full Metal Jacket'*

"Are you allowed to *eat* jelly donuts, Private Pyle?" - *Drill Instructor Gunnery Sergeant Hartman (R. Lee Ermey) in 'Full Metal Jacket'*

"I'll make life-takers and heartbreakers out of them, sir." - *Gunnery Sergeant Tom Highway (played by Clint Eastwood) in the film 'Heartbreak Ridge'*

"You may not believe it, but under fire 'Animal Mother' is one of the finest human beings in the world. All he needs is someone to throw hand grenades at him for the rest of his life." - *'Eight Ball' in 'Full Metal Jacket'*

"I eat breakfast three-hundred yards from four-thousand Cubans who are trained to kill me, so don't think you can come down here, flash your badge, and make me nervous." - *Colonel Nathan Jessup (portrayed by Jack Nicholson) in 'A Few Good Men'*

"Did your parents have any children that lived?" - *Drill Instructor Gunnery Sergeant Hartman (R. Lee Ermey) in 'Full Metal Jacket'*

"I don't like the name Lawrence. Only faggots and sailors are named Lawrence. From now on your name is Gomer Pyle!" - *Drill Instructor Gunnery Sergeant Hartman (R. Lee Ermey) in 'Full Metal Jacket'*

"Private Pyle, what are you trying to do to my beloved Corps?" - *Drill Instructor Gunnery Sergeant Hartman (R. Lee Ermey) in 'Full Metal Jacket'*

"Your ass looks like one-hundred and fifty pounds of chewed bubble gum Pyle, did you know that? – *Drill Instructor Gunnery Sergeant Hartman (R. Lee Ermey) in 'Full Metal Jacket'*

"I like all you Navy boys. Every time we have to go somewhere to fight, you fellas always give us a ride." - *Lieutenant Kendrick (Kiefer Sutherland) in 'A Few Good Men'*

"If the Army and the Navy, ever look on Heaven's scenes, they will find the streets are guarded, by United States Marines!" - *From 'The Marines' Hymn'*

"They call me Mac. The name's unimportant. You can best identify me by the six chevrons, three up and three down, and by that row of hashmarks. Thirty years in the United States Marine Corps." - *From Leon Uris' bestselling book 'Battle Cry'*

"They came from America's cities and farms and reservations - boys who became men under the withering fire of a bold and terrible enemy. In Pacific killing zones called Tarawa and Guadalcanal, they stared into the savage face of war and did not flinch. In their country's most desperate hour - in the blood, anguish, and terror of combat - they would grow to be comrades, soldiers, heroes, Marines. This is their story." - *From Leon Uris' bestselling book 'Battle Cry'*

QUOTES BY OR ABOUT
"ANTI-PATRIOTS"

The Lore of the Corps

"When the eagles are silent, the parrots begin to jabber."
- *Sir Winston Churchill*

"Congressmen who willfully take actions during wartime that damage morale and undermine the military are saboteurs and should be arrested, exiled, or hanged."
- *President Abraham Lincoln (sometimes I wish Honest Abe was still in the White House...)*

"Remember, Benedict Arnold was awarded several medals for valor by the Continental Congress, but it does not make him any less a traitor." - *Alan H. Gibson, referring to John Kerry*

"An appeaser is one who feeds a crocodile, hoping it will eat him last." - *Winston Churchill*

"A disturbingly large number of entertainers have abused their celebrity status, and need to learn being *famous* does not necessarily make them *smart*. Exactly who appointed Sean Penn Secretary of State, anyway?"
- *Master Sergeant Andy Bufalo, USMC (Ret)*

"Jane Fonda is of course the benchmark by which all (modern day) traitors are measured. She went *way* beyond voicing her opinions when she traveled to North Vietnam for a photo-op sitting at the controls of an active anti-aircraft gun." - *Master Sergeant Andy Bufalo, USMC*

"To the best of my knowledge the only one in that entire group (unpatriotic Hollywood 'celebrities') who has served in uniform is Jane Fonda – although as we all know *that* uniform belonged to the North Vietnamese Army." - *Master Sergeant Andy Bufalo, USMC (Ret)*

"Martin Sheen of the television show *The West Wing* is another idiot with delusions of relevance. His 'I'm not the President, but I play one on TV' mentality is scary. Someone needs to tell this man the foreign policy briefings he has been getting are *fake*." - *Master Sergeant Andy Bufalo, USMC (Ret)*

"It's all of our jobs to keep our minds as expansive as possible. If you can see [the terrorists] as a relative who's dangerously sick, and we have to give them medicine, and the medicine is love and compassion. There's nothing better." – *Actor Richard Gere*

"We have been the cowards, lobbing cruise missiles from 2,000 miles away. That's cowardly. Staying in the airplane when it hits the building - say what you want about it, it's not cowardly." - *Bill Maher after the 9/11 terrorist attacks.*

"The First Amendment not only applies to liberals who speak out against the government, but to those who call them traitors as well. If anything, grunts have *more* of a right to free speech since they are the ones who put their butts on the line!" – *Master Sergeant Andy Bufalo, USMC*

"The passengers were scaredy-cats because they were mostly white. If the passengers had included black men, those killers, with their puny bodies and unimpressive small knives, would have been crushed by the dudes." – *Michael Moore talking about the heroes of Flight 93*

"Some men are alive simply because it is against the law to kill them." - *Edward W. Howe*

AXIOMS & UNCLASSIFIED NUGGETS OF WISDOM

The Lore of the Corps

"Proper Prior Planning Prevents Piss Poor Performance!" – *The Seven "Ps"*

"When in doubt, empty your magazine!"

"The more you sweat in peace, the less you bleed in war!"

"A 'sucking chest wound' is nature's way of telling you it's time to slow down."

"Payback is a Medevac!"

"That [state] which separates its scholars from its warriors will have its thinking done by cowards, and its fighting by fools."- *Thucydides, 'The Peloponnesian Wars'*

"Anyone can be a civilian – you don't even have to take a physical!"

"There are very few problems in the world which cannot be solved by a suitable application of high explosives."

"A journey of a thousand miles begins with one step… and a *lot* of bitching."

"I'm not worried about the bullet with my name on it. I'm worried about the millions that say 'to whom it may concern.'"

"Mind over matter. If you don't mind, it doesn't matter!"

"The only easy day… was yesterday!" - *USMC Axiom*

"I'd rather be lucky than good!" - *Words to live by*

"Luck is when preparation meets opportunity!"

"Whoever said the pen is mightier than the sword obviously never encountered automatic weapons."
- *General MacArthur*

"A letter of reprimand is better than no mail at all."
- *Spray-painted on the side of a tent in Vietnam*

"... the twin pillars of political correctness are willful ignorance and a steadfast refusal to face the truth..."
- *George MacDonald Fraser*

"A prisoner of war is a man who tries to kill you and fails, and then asks *you* not to kill *him*." - *Sir Winston Churchill*

"A corpsman is usually a young, long-haired, bearded, Marine-hatin' Sailor with certain medical skills, who will go through the very gates of hell to get to a wounded Marine."- *Major H. G. 'Dunk' Duncan USMC (Ret)*

"Live as if you were to die tomorrow. Learn as if you were to live forever." - *Mahatma Gandhi*

"To err is human, to forgive divine – neither of which is Marine Corps policy!"

"To walk my post from flank to flank, and take no crap from any rank!" - *Unofficial Twelfth General Order*

"You've gotta *love* it – just *liking* it isn't going to get you through the day!"

"The only thing harder than being a Marine is being married to one." - *Colonel "Irish" Egan USMC*

"Marines are different. They have a different outlook on life."

"All men are created equal – and then some become Marines."

"With the help of God and a few Marines..."

"And on the eighth day, God created Marines..."

"Join the Navy and see the world - join the Marine Corps and police it!"

"Sleep well tonight – the Marines are on duty!"

"It's hard to be humble, when you are the finest!"

"Heaven won't take us, and Hell's afraid we'll take over!"

"USMC: When it absolutely, positively must be destroyed overnight."

"Marines don't have an attitude problem; we are just *that* good."

"Nobody ever promised you a rose garden."
– *USMC Recruiting Poster*

"Once a Marine, always a Marine!"

"Sweat dries, blood clots, bones heal. Suck it up. Be a Marine!"

"Nobody ever drowned in sweat."

"If *anybody* could get in, it wouldn't be the Marine Corps!"

"When the going gets tough, the tough... call the Marines!"

"Gung Ho!" - *Term brought back from China by Colonel Evans Carlson which later became the motto of the Marine Raiders*

"The Marine Corps *is* part of the Department of the Navy... the *Men's* Department!"

"Death before Dishonor!" - *tattoo on the arm of John Basilone*

"You can be in the Army, you can join the Air Force, but you *become* a Marine."

"Pain is weakness leaving the body."

"Marines do not want to go in harm's way without their corpsmen, and corpsmen do not want their Marines to go in harm's way without *them*."

"Ever wonder why the Marine Corps doesn't have a football team like the Army, Navy and Air Force? We're here to protect a *country*, not a quarterback."
- *USMC Recruiting Poster*

"This isn't Burger King. You get it my way, or you don't get it at all!" - *Sign behind the desk of a Marine First Sergeant*

"You are either a warrior, or you are not!"

The Lore of the Corps

Breinigsville, PA USA
11 January 2011
253136BV00004B/22/P